Good Girl Deprogramming

TEEN EDITION

MICHELLE MINNIKIN & CAROLINE BOWMER

Copyright © 2026 by Michelle Minnikin & Caroline Bowmer

All rights reserved. No part of this publication may be reproduced, distributed or transmitted in any form or by any means without permission of the publisher, except in the case of brief quotations referencing the body of work and in accordance with copyright law.

The information given in this book should not be treated as a substitute for professional medical advice; always consult a medical practitioner. Any use of information in this book is at the reader's discretion and risk. Neither the author nor the publisher can be held responsible for any loss, claim or damage arising out of the use, or misuse, of the suggestions made, the failure to take medical advice or for any material on third party websites.

Good Girl Deprogramming® is a registered trademark of The Deprogramming Company Ltd.

ISBN: 978-1-9194380-0-9

Cover & interior design by Lynda Mangoro.
inkandalchemy.studio

www.deprogramming.company
www.alchemy-education.com

For Lizzie.

With love, always. — *Caroline*

And for our inner 10-year-olds.

We wish we'd had this book back then.

But we have it now - and so do you. — *Michelle*

Contents

Welcome	7
Chapter 1: What Is Good Girl Conditioning?	15
Chapter 2: What Is Coercive Control?	33
Chapter 3: Too Trusting?	43
Chapter 4: Doing Everything By Yourself	53
Chapter 5: When Girls Are Mean to Girls	63
Chapter 6: Is It Me or Am I Just Confused?	75
Chapter 7: Tired All the Time	85
Chapter 8: Trying to Be Perfect	95
Chapter 9: Your Body Is Not the Problem	105
Chapter 10: The Should Monster	119
Chapter 11: Please Like Me!	129
Chapter 12: Not Feeling Strong	141
Chapter 13: Feeling Worried All the Time	151
Chapter 14: Am I Ever Good Enough?	159
Chapter 15: Safety & Consent Toolkit	169
Chapter 16: You Don't Have to Earn It	179
A Note From Us	183
Acknowledgements	184

Welcome

Hey you,

Thanks for picking up this book.

You might be here because someone gave it to you. Or maybe you found it and something about the cover, or the title, or the idea of not always having to be a "Good Girl" made you feel curious.

Whatever brought you here, welcome. (This space is yours.)

You don't have to impress anyone while you read this. You don't have to take notes unless you want to. You don't have to be brave every single second. You don't even have to agree with everything. This book is not a test. It's not a list of rules. It's a space for you to think, wonder, scribble, question, reflect, and be real.

You might laugh at some bits. You might feel angry at others. You might think, "Wait... that's me." Or "That sounds like someone I know." Or even "I've never thought about it that way before."

All of that is good.

The only thing you need to bring is yourself. Your messy, curious, brilliant self. You don't need to be perfect. You don't need to be good all the time. You are already enough.

So let's get started. We're going to talk about things you've probably felt but maybe never had words for. We're going to figure out what you've been taught, what you want to keep, and what you're ready to let go of.

You're not alone in this. There are lots of girls doing this work too. Some older, some younger. Some just beginning. Some a little further along. But all of them trying to live their lives with more freedom, honesty and joy.

And now, you are one of them.

Let's go.

 **WORDS TO KNOW**

Sometimes this book uses big or new words. That's OK! Here's a little guide to help you understand what they mean. You can come back here any time.

✧ Good Girl Conditioning
    The invisible rules and messages girls are taught from a young age about how to behave, look, and feel - usually to keep others happy, not themselves.

✧ Conditioning
    A way people are trained or taught, often without even realising it. Like how dogs learn to sit when given a treat - but with people, it can be much sneakier.

✧ Coercive Control
    A type of control where someone uses sneaky tricks - like guilt, fear, rules, or praise - to get you to do what they want. It can happen in friendships, families, or even in society.

◇ Deprogramming
Unlearning rules or ideas that were given to you but don't feel right anymore. It's about thinking for yourself and choosing what's true for you.

◇ Boundaries
The limits you set to protect yourself. Like saying "no" when something doesn't feel right or taking time for yourself when you need it.

◇ People Pleasing
Doing things just to make others happy, even if it makes you feel sad, tired, or invisible.

◇ Patriarchy
A system where men have more power than women in families, schools, jobs, and laws. It affects how people are treated and what's expected of them.

◇ Stereotype
A simple idea people believe about a group - like "girls are emotional" or "boys don't cry" - that isn't always true and can be unfair.

◇ Internalised
When you start to believe something you've heard a lot - even if it's not true or helpful. Like thinking you have to be perfect to be loved.

✧ Power
The ability to make choices, speak up, and shape your life - or influence what happens around you.

✧ Voice
Not just speaking out loud, but sharing your truth, ideas, feelings, and needs in a way that feels right for you.

✧ Agency
Your right and ability to make decisions about your own life.

✧ Shame
That awful feeling of being "not good enough" or "too much." It often shows up when we think we've broken a rule or let someone down.

HOW TO USE THIS BOOK

This is your book. That means you get to decide how to use it.

* ✵ You can start at the beginning and move through it one chapter at a time.
* ✵ You can start at the end and work backwards.
* ✵ You can flick through the pages and choose the bits that speak to you.
* ✵ There's no wrong way to do this.

You don't have to fill in every page or do every activity.
Some pages might make you think. Some might make you feel.
Some might make you want to skip ahead - and that's totally OK.

This workbook is here to help you notice, unlearn and grow.
You get to take what you need, leave what you don't, and come back any time.

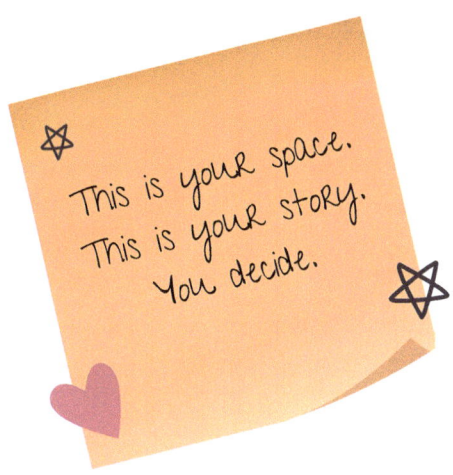

FEELING BIG FEELINGS? HERE'S YOUR SAFETY NET

Some parts of this book might make you feel confused, upset, or just full of questions. That's OK. Big feelings can show up when you start to notice things you hadn't seen before - especially if they've been affecting you for a long time.

You don't have to figure it all out on your own.

If something feels too heavy, or if you're not sure what to do with a feeling, talk to someone you trust. This could be:

- A parent, grandparent or carer
- A trusted teacher or school counsellor
- An older sibling or cousin
- A friend's parent
- A youth group leader or coach
- A helpline or support organisation

You are not a burden. Asking for help is brave and smart. And no matter what you're feeling — you are not alone.

⭐ NOTE FOR CAREGIVERS

This book has a companion resource designed just for you: *the Caregivers Companion*. While your young person is exploring the ideas in this book, you'll have your own guide to support their journey - and yours. It offers insights, reflection questions, and tools to help you understand what they're learning, start meaningful conversations, and support them as they unlearn limiting messages and grow into their full selves.

We believe this journey is more powerful when shared. *The Teen Edition* and the *Caregivers Companion* are meant to be read alongside each other - or at your own pace - so you both feel supported, understood, and empowered.

You can download it for free at:
www.michelleminnikin.com/caregiver-companion

⭐ ACTIVITY: SPOT YOUR STRENGTHS

Let's start with what's already great

Before we go any further, let's take a moment to notice the amazing things about you - the parts of yourself that you're proud of, the things that make you you.

Write or draw 3 things you like about yourself. They can be anything - the way you care for your friends, your sense of humour, how creative you are, how you bounce back when things go wrong, or even how you think deeply about things.

You don't need to be perfect. You don't need to be the best. These are your strengths - the ones that are already in you.

1 _____

_____

2 _____

_____

3 _____

_____

> Remember: these are the things the Good Girl voice might try to make you forget. But they're yours. Keep them close.

CHAPTER 1
What Is Good Girl Conditioning?

You've probably heard the phrase "Good Girl" before.

Maybe it was said with a smile when you helped someone. Maybe it was whispered when someone wanted you to stay quiet. Maybe it was shouted when someone thought you'd done something wrong.

Sometimes being called a "Good Girl" feels nice - like someone's proud of you. Other times it feels uncomfortable, like you're supposed to follow rules you didn't choose, just to keep everyone else happy.

That's what this chapter is about. The Rules. The ones you never really agreed to, but somehow still feel like you have to follow.

 So... WHAT IS GOOD GIRL CONDITIONING?

Let's break it down.

Conditioning is a word used in psychology. It means the way people are taught or trained - usually without even realising it.

And Good Girl Conditioning is all the invisible training girls get from a young age about how to act, look, speak, feel, and behave in order to be liked, accepted, praised, or seen as "good".

It can sound like:

"BE NICE."

"DON'T BE BOSSY."

"SMILE, LOVE."

"DON'T MAKE A FUSS."

"SAY SORRY."

"DON'T TALK BACK."

"BE QUIET."

"THAT'S NOT VERY LADYLIKE."

"YOU'RE TOO MUCH."

"YOU'RE TOO SENSITIVE."

"JUST BE GRATEFUL.

The rules don't always come with instructions, but they're there. In what you're praised for. In what you're criticised for. In how girls are talked about in class, in families, on TV, and online.

 WHAT IT FEELS LIKE

Good Girl Conditioning can show up like:

- Smiling when you don't want to
- Saying "yes" when you mean "no"
- Worrying more about how others feel than how you feel
- Trying to be perfect all the time
- Feeling guilty for taking up space
- Apologising when you haven't done anything wrong
- Pretending to be OK when you're not
- Feeling like you need to earn love or approval

And you might not even realise it's happening. That's what makes it so sneaky.

⭐ BUT WAIT – ISN'T BEING A GOOD PERSON... GOOD?

Yes! Kindness, honesty, respect, and care are all important. But there's a difference between:

➡ **Being a good person** = You choose your actions because they feel right and true for you.

➡ **Being a "Good Girl"** = You do what's expected of you to please others, avoid conflict, or be accepted, even when it doesn't feel right.

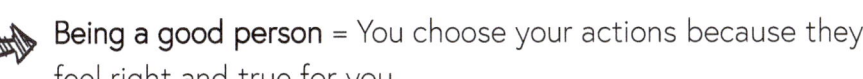

This book isn't telling you to stop being kind or caring. It's about helping you figure out why you do what you do, and whether those choices are really yours.

QUICK REFLECTION

Grab your pen or just think it through…

1. Have you ever done something you didn't want to, just so someone would like you more?

2. What do you think people expect "Good Girls" to act like?

3. What happens when girls don't follow those rules?

WHERE DOES THIS ALL COME FROM?

The pressure to be a Good Girl doesn't come from one person. It comes from EVERYWHERE. From our culture, all the ways we're shaped by family, school, religion, media, tradition, and even social media.

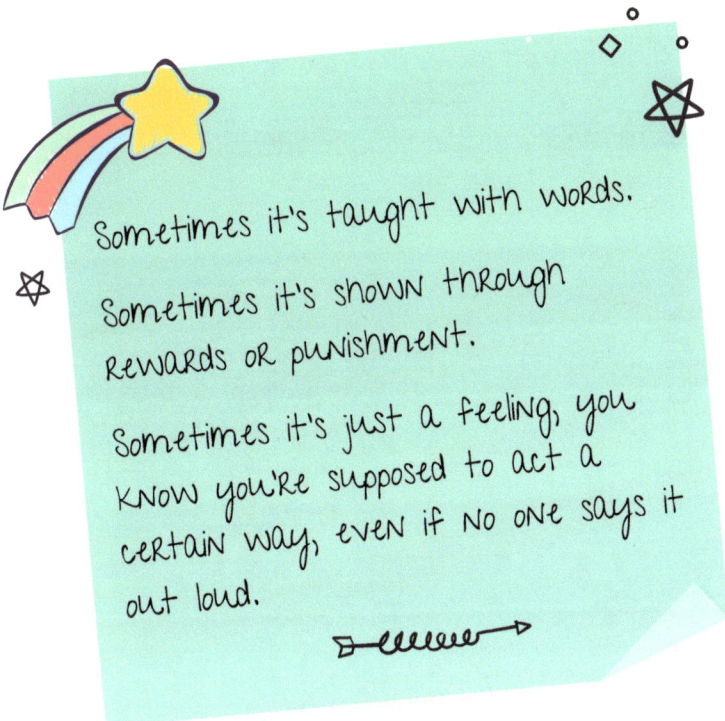

Sometimes it's taught with words.

Sometimes it's shown through rewards or punishment.

Sometimes it's just a feeling, you know you're supposed to act a certain way, even if no one says it out loud.

And the truth is, everyone is trained in some way. Boys too. But girls often get a very specific message: Be good. Be small. Be nice. Don't make people uncomfortable.

This book is here to help you notice those messages. Not so you can throw a tantrum or burn everything down (though a little rebellion is healthy). But so you can choose what you want to keep, and what you're ready to let go of.

ONE SIZE DOESN'T FIT ALL

Not all girls experience Good Girl Conditioning in the same way. Things like your race, religion, family background, culture, disability, or whether you're neurodivergent can change how these rules show up in your life. Some girls are told to be quiet in one way, others in a completely different way. Some are judged more harshly, or made to feel "too different" just for being themselves.

This book tries to talk about the common patterns, but your story might have extra layers - and that matters.

Every part of who you are is important. You deserve to feel seen, safe, and strong, exactly as you are.

 WHY THIS MATTERS: FREEDOM OVER FITTING IN

What's the point of all this? Why does it matter?

Great question.

Here's the thing:
So many girls are trained to fit in instead of figure out who they are.
To be good instead of true.
To be liked instead of free.
And that training can stick.
It can quietly shape your choices.
It can make you second-guess yourself.
It can make you think being tired, anxious or small is just "normal".

But you weren't born to play small.

> You were born to be real.
> To think your own thoughts.
> To take up space.
> To make noise, ask questions, and feel all your feelings.
> To rest without guilt, to speak without apology, to say No with confidence.

SO WHAT HAPPENS IF YOU DON'T?

If you never stop and question the Good Girl messages you've picked up, they might end up running your life.

You might:

- Keep quiet when you really want to speak up
- Say yes when everything in you wants to say no
- Push yourself until you're exhausted, just to prove you're "enough"
- Believe you have to earn rest, love, approval
- Stay in friendships or situations that make you feel small
- Keep thinking, "I just need to try harder," instead of asking, "Why am I carrying all this?"

And the truth is — it's not your fault.
But it is in your power to change it.

WHAT YOU GET WHEN YOU DEPROGRAMME

When you start to unlearn what you were told you should be…

You start to notice who you really are.

You begin to:

Feel more grounded and sure of yourself.
Ask questions instead of blindly agreeing.
Choose things that actually fit you.
Make mistakes, and grow from them.
Know your worth without needing to prove it.
Rest, speak, create, dream, and take up space without guilt.
You stop trying to squeeze into a box that was never made for you.
And you start becoming someone even you are proud of.

THE POINT ISN'T TO BE PERFECT. THE POINT IS TO BE FREE.

Deprogramming isn't about getting it all right.
It's about noticing the invisible rules, and deciding which ones you want to keep.

This work is about your freedom.
Your joy. Your choices. Your voice.

> Because your life shouldN't be a peRfoRmaNce.
> It should be youRs.

Write one reason why you're doing this workbook. What do you want to feel more of?

 # YOUR POWER

The moment you notice the conditioning is the moment it starts to lose its power.

> You don't have to follow every rule someone gave you.
>
> You don't have to be everything for everyone.
>
> You don't have to be "good" all the time to be worthy of love, care and respect.

You are allowed to take up space. You are allowed to question things. You are allowed to choose yourself.

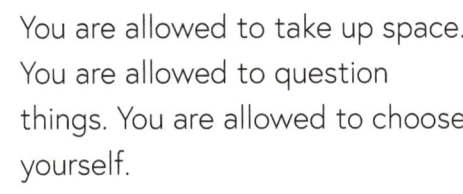

This chapter is the start of all of that.

 **REFLECTION PROMPTS**

These can be written, drawn, or discussed aloud, depending on what works for you.

1. The Rules I've Learned

Write down (or draw) three things you've been told about how girls are "supposed" to behave. Where did each one come from? Do you agree with it?

EXAMPLE: "GIRLS SHOULD BE QUIET" – I HEARD THIS AT SCHOOL.

Do I agree? No, because sometimes I have something important to say.

1. _____

2. _____

3. _____

2. When I Pretended to Be OK

Think of a time when you smiled, said yes, or stayed quiet even though you didn't really want to. What did you feel in your body? What do you wish you could have said or done instead?

----

3. The "Good Girl" Voice in My Head

Draw or describe what that voice sounds like. What does it say to you when you're about to speak up, take a risk, or say no?

Now, write a reply back to it. What would the brave, kind, real version of you say?

 VISUAL ACTIVITY: REWRITING THE RULEBOOK

The Good Girl Rulebook (and what I'm doing with it)

Draw an imaginary book called "The Good Girl Rulebook". On one side of the page, write or sketch what's inside it.

Examples:

- BE QUIET
- ALWAYS SAY SORRY
- DON'T GET ANGRY
- MAKE EVERYONE HAPPY

On the other side, redesign the rulebook your way. What new rules (or un-rules) would you include?

Examples:

- SPEAK WHEN YOU HAVE SOMETHING TO SAY
- SAY SORRY ONLY WHEN YOU MEAN IT
- ANGER IS ALLOWED
- YOU DON'T HAVE TO PLEASE EVERYONE

SPOT IT: REAL-LIFE GOOD GIRL MOMENTS

Create a "spotting list" of Good Girl messages in books, films, school, social media or everyday life. Write them down, draw them, or keep a log for a few days.

Ask:

What was said or shown?
What did the girl or woman do?
What message was being sent?
Do I agree with it?

Optional: Share one with a friend or adult and talk about how it made you feel.

CLOSING PROMPT: WHAT DO I WANT TO KEEP?

Not all parts of being thoughtful or kind are bad. But the goal is to choose, not just follow.

Ask:

* What qualities do I really like about myself?
* Which ones do I feel I've been taught to have to make others comfortable?
* What's one rule I'm ready to let go of?

CHAPTER 2
What Is Coercive Control?

Before we get into it, we want to tell you a little bit about one of the co-authors, Michelle.

When Michelle was growing up, she was smart, kind, and creative, but also loud, impulsive, and intense. She had big feelings. She asked too many questions. She said what she thought. She was, in the words some adults used, *a bit much*.

She didn't know it then, but she had ADHD. That meant her brain moved quickly, her feelings were strong, and her energy didn't always match what the world expected from a "good girl".

Instead of being helped, she was told to tone it down. Be quieter. Stop interrupting. Be more polite. Smile more. She was never quite getting it right.

After a while, she learned to hide the parts of herself that got her into trouble. She tried to be easier. Softer. Smaller. More "good".

She didn't know this had a name. She just thought it was what she had to do to be liked and stay safe.

Later, as an adult, Michelle learned about something called **coercive control** - a way people shape and manage others using guilt, pressure, shame or confusion.

It hit her like a wave. Because even though no one had yelled at her or told her exactly what to do, she had been trained to ignore herself in order to make other people more comfortable.

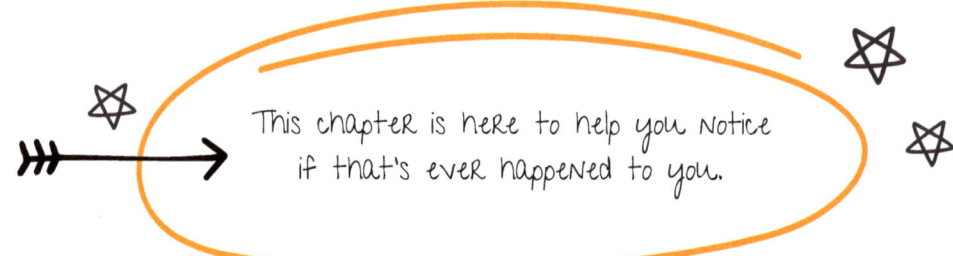

This chapter is here to help you notice if that's ever happened to you.

 ## WHAT IS COERCIVE CONTROL?

Coercive control is when someone uses **emotional pressure**, not physical force, to control how another person behaves.

It might not look like "bullying". It might not sound like shouting. But it works quietly, like a fog, making you feel unsure of yourself. It's when someone slowly teaches you that keeping them happy is more important than listening to your own feelings.

A GROWN-UP WORD, EXPLAINED SIMPLY

There's a social scientist named **Albert Biderman** who once studied how prisoners were controlled, without force, just by using emotional and psychological pressure. He listed the tools that made people feel small, helpless, or confused enough to give in.

Those same tools are used, often without anyone realising, on girls (and women) every day.

Not by villains. Sometimes by people who seem kind, or who say they love us. Sometimes even by people who believe they're doing what's best.

But the effect is the same: we learn to **doubt ourselves, overthink everything, and give our power away.**

⭐ THE TOOLS OF COERCIVE CONTROL

Here's how it shows up - at school, in families, in friendships, online.

1 Isolation

You're slowly pulled away from people who support you.

> "DON'T TELL ANYONE."
>
> "NO ONE ELSE WOULD UNDERSTAND."
>
> "YOU'RE NOT LIKE OTHER GIRLS."

2 Exhaustion

You're kept busy, worried, overwhelmed - so you don't have time to question it.

> "YOU NEED TO DO BETTER."
>
> "IF YOU TRY HARDER, THIS WILL STOP."
>
> "DON'T LET ANYONE DOWN."

3 Ever-Changing Rules

You never quite know what's expected. What was OK yesterday isn't OK today.

> "YOU SHOULD'VE KNOWN BETTER."
>
> "YOU'RE TOO MUCH."
>
> "NOW YOU'RE TOO QUIET."

4 Selective Kindness

You're praised when you do what's expected - but ignored or punished when you don't.

> "I'M PROUD OF YOU... NOW THAT YOU'RE BEHAVING."
>
> "YOU'RE LOVELY WHEN YOU'RE NOT SO MOODY."

5 Shame and Blame

You're made to feel like you're the problem - even when you haven't done anything wrong.

> "YOU'RE SO DRAMATIC."
>
> "THIS IS WHY NO ONE WANTS TO HANG OUT WITH YOU."
>
> "STOP MAKING EVERYTHING ABOUT YOU."

6 Threats

Even subtle ones - like being left out, embarrassed, or made fun of if you don't go along.

> "IF YOU DON'T SEND IT, I'LL TELL EVERYONE."
>
> "FINE, DON'T COME. JUST DON'T EXPECT ME TO INVITE YOU AGAIN."

 **WHAT IT FEELS LIKE**

If someone is using coercive control, you might feel:

- **Confused** (like you never know where you stand)
- **Guilty** (like it's always your fault)
- **Tense** (like you're walking on eggshells)
- **Drained** (like you're always trying to please someone)
- **Trapped** (like saying no would make everything worse)

You might also:

Say sorry all the time

Stop trusting your feelings

Think, "If I just behave, maybe this will go away"

These are signs that someone's using power in a way that isn't safe or kind - even if they're not raising their voice or breaking rules.

 ## A QUICK EXAMPLE

Let's say you tell a friend you can't come to a shopping trip today because you need a break. They say:

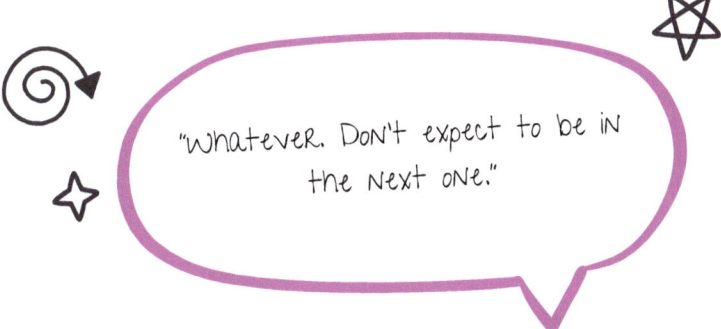

"Whatever. Don't expect to be in the next one."

They didn't shout. But now you feel bad, maybe even scared that you'll be left out.

That's pressure. That's control. That's not what friendship is supposed to feel like.

⭐ **WHAT YOU CAN DO**

1. Notice it

Naming what's happening is powerful.

You might say: *"This feels like pressure, not care."*

2. Trust your gut

If something feels off, you don't need permission to step away.

3. Talk to a trusted adult

You don't have to handle this alone. You can tell someone - even if you're scared.

4. Set a boundary

You can say:

"I don't feel OK with this."

"I need space."

"I'm not comfortable with this friendship right now."

 REFLECTION PROMPTS

* Has anyone ever made you feel like you were "too much" just for being yourself?

* Do you ever feel like you're walking on eggshells around someone?

* Who makes you feel safe, steady and like you can be your whole self?

ACTIVITY: KNOW THE SIGNS

Make a table with two columns:

Feels Controlling	Feels Respectful
I feel scared to say no	I feel safe to be honest
They make me feel guilty	They ask what I need
I never know what they want	I know I can make mistakes

Add your own examples. Come back to it whenever you feel unsure.

⭐ FINAL MESSAGE

You do not have to be controlled to be loved.

You do not have to stay quiet to stay safe.

You are not "too much" – you were never too much.

The more you understand coercive control, the more power you get back.

And you deserve all of it.

CHAPTER 3
Too Trusting?

Being kind doesn't mean believing everything, or everyone.

Maya liked being the nice one.

She wasn't loud or dramatic. She didn't want attention. She just wanted people to feel included - especially in the new group of friends she'd made in Year 8.

There were four of them. They had a group chat where they sent TikToks, inside jokes, homework reminders, and the odd message about who was annoying them that day. Maya didn't always agree with the gossip, but she didn't want to be the one to make a fuss.

One afternoon, something different popped up. A message from one of the girls, followed by a photo. It wasn't a meme. It wasn't funny. It made Maya's stomach twist.

She knew what she was looking at wasn't okay - and that it definitely wasn't meant to be shared.

No one replied straight away.

Then someone laughed about it.

Then another girl forwarded it.

And Maya just… stayed quiet.

She wanted to believe it wasn't a big deal. That if the others thought it was fine, maybe it was. That if she said something, she'd make it worse - or be pushed out of the group completely.

But deep down, she knew.

It was wrong.

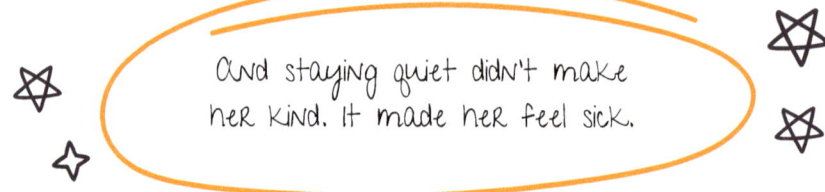

And staying quiet didn't make her kind. It made her feel sick.

Later, the school found out.

There were serious consequences. Phones taken. Parents called. People crying in corridors.

Maya wasn't the one who started it - but she had watched it happen. And even though she hadn't meant to hurt anyone, she had.

For the first time, she realised that being kind doesn't mean going along with everything.

Trust has to be earned. And sometimes, real kindness means being brave enough to say: "This isn't okay."

This story is for you if:

* You've stayed quiet to avoid conflict, even when something felt wrong.
* You believe being kind means not causing drama.
* You worry that standing up for what's right will make you lose friends.

 # LET'S TALK ABOUT TRUST

Trust is a good thing. In fact, it's one of the most powerful things you can offer someone. But here's what no one always tells you:

Trust should be earned, not automatic.

You can be a kind, open-hearted person and still take time to ask questions. You don't have to believe everything you're told. You don't have to go along with something just because everyone else is.

Being too trusting isn't a flaw, it's something many girls are taught.

You might hear:

The truth is: You can ask questions and still be respectful. You can say no and still be kind. You can trust your gut even when everyone else is saying something different.

 CRITICAL THINKING

Critical thinking means learning to pause, reflect, and ask:

- "Is this true?"
- "Does this feel right to me?"
- "Who benefits if I believe this?"

> It's like a mental superpower that helps you decide for yourself what makes sense, instead of just going along with what others say.

WHAT IT FEELS LIKE TO BE "TOO TRUSTING"

- Saying "yes" too quickly, even when something feels off
- Feeling scared to disagree in case someone gets upset
- Believing everything someone says, even if they've hurt you before

- Feeling guilty for asking questions

- Worrying that saying no makes you a "bad friend" or "difficult"

If any of that sounds familiar, you're not alone. And it's not your fault.

It just means you're ready to practise something new: thoughtful, brave, kind questioning.

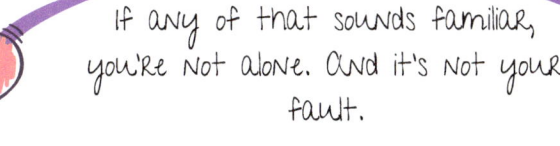 YOUR INNER QUESTION-ASKER

Imagine a part of you, a quiet voice inside, that's allowed to ask questions.

Not to be rude. Not to start arguments.

Just to check. To stay safe. To think for yourself.

You might not hear that voice loudly at first. But it's there.

And every time you listen to it, it grows stronger.

 ## DEPROGRAMMING TOOLS

* **Don't believe everything you're told:** Ask: Where did this come from? Is it true?

* **Don't believe everything you think:** Feelings are real, but not always facts.

* **Ask:** Who benefits if I believe this? Who might be left out if I don't question it?

* **Read or listen to different people:** Think: Could another version of this be true?

* **Keep reflecting:** Try journaling, spider diagrams, or curiosity lists.

* **Ask:** What have I changed my mind about recently? What helped me grow?

⭐ REFLECTION PROMPTS

1. Have you ever believed someone too quickly? What happened?

2. When has your gut feeling told you something was off?

3. What questions do you wish you'd asked in a tricky moment?

 ACTIVITY: MY CURIOUS BRAIN

Draw a brain in the middle of your page.

Around it, write as many questions as you can think of that help you stay thoughtful and aware.

Examples:

- WHAT DO I REALLY THINK ABOUT THIS?
- IS THIS TRUE FOR EVERYONE, OR JUST FOR SOME PEOPLE?
- WHAT'S MY INSTINCT SAYING RIGHT NOW?
- WHERE DID THIS IDEA COME FROM?

Give your curious brain a name if you want. It's part of your power.

⭐ FINAL MESSAGE

Being curious doesn't mean being mean.

Saying no doesn't mean you're rude.

Asking questions doesn't make you difficult.

It makes you strong. It makes you wise. It makes you you.

You don't have to believe everything. You just have to believe in your right to check.

Bob, the too-trusting Clownfish

CHAPTER 4
Doing Everything By Yourself

You don't have to carry it all. You're allowed to ask.

Avaani's revision planner was beautiful.

Colour-coded. Timed to the minute. Pages of neat, printed schedules.

She had cancelled dance, skipped sleepovers and turned down every weekend plan for the last two months.

Everyone thought she was doing great.

Inside?

> SHE WAS EXHAUSTED. HER HEAD ACHED. SHE KEPT FORGETTING WHAT DAY IT WAS.

And the worst part?

SHE STILL FELT BEHIND.

It didn't matter how many hours she studied, her brain wouldn't hold onto things. She'd read a page, then read it again, and still not remember it the next morning. She kept telling herself, *Work harder. Push more. No one else is going to do it for you.*

Then she started crying one day in the middle of her Spanish notes.

No big meltdown. Just quiet, frustrating tears that made the ink run.

And that's when something clicked.

She didn't need to do this all by herself.

She didn't have to be the "strong one" who never asked for help.

So she did. She asked.

This chapter is for every girl who's carrying too much and still thinks she's not doing enough.

You are not weak for needing support.

You are human. And you deserve to breathe.

This story is for you if:

- ✱ You push yourself to exhaustion trying to do everything perfectly.
- ✱ You find it hard to admit when you're struggling.
- ✱ You think asking for help means you've failed.

⭐ LET'S TALK ABOUT ASKING FOR HELP

A lot of girls are taught that independence is a strength. And it is.

But somewhere along the way, that can turn into something else:

- "DON'T BE NEEDY."
- "OTHER PEOPLE HAVE IT WORSE."
- "IF I JUST TRY HARDER, I CAN COPE."
- "NO ONE ELSE IS STRUGGLING, SO I SHOULDN'T BE EITHER."

The truth is, being able to ask for help is also a strength. One of the biggest. It takes bravery. Honesty. And trust.

You are not a burden. You are not weak. You are a human being.

You don't have to earn support. You deserve it just by being you.

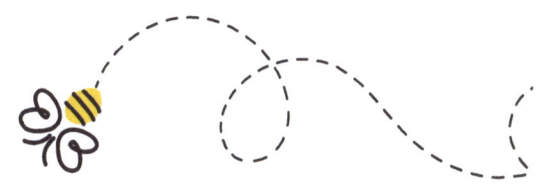

 WHY WE HIDE IT

Sometimes we don't ask for help because:

- ✧ WE'RE SCARED OF LOOKING LIKE WE'VE FAILED
- ✧ WE DON'T WANT TO BE A PROBLEM
- ✧ WE THINK WE SHOULD BE ABLE TO COPE
- ✧ WE DON'T WANT TO MAKE THINGS AWKWARD
- ✧ WE DON'T EVEN KNOW HOW TO ASK
- ✧ WE DON'T THINK WE DESERVE HELP

But keeping it all inside doesn't make it better. It just makes us lonelier.

And one day, all the things we've been carrying by ourselves might get too heavy.

⭐ WHAT IT FEELS LIKE TO CARRY IT ALONE

- ○ Tired, even after sleeping
- ○ Snappy or withdrawn
- ○ Saying "I'm fine" but not meaning it
- ○ Feeling like no one really sees you
- ○ Wanting someone to help, but not knowing how to say it

You don't have to wait until you're overwhelmed to speak up.

You're allowed to ask early. To ask small. To ask often.

A NEW KIND OF STRENGTH

Real strength is knowing your limits. It's knowing when to rest, when to reach out, and when to let someone walk beside you.

You don't lose anything by asking for help. You gain space. You gain clarity. You gain connection.

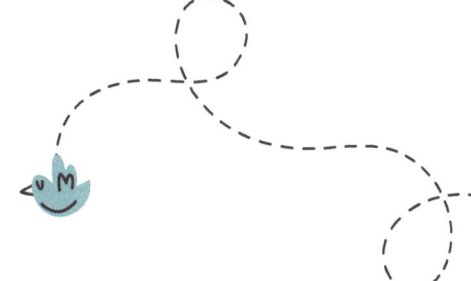

DEPROGRAMMING TOOLS

* Make a "Support Squad" list: Who are five people you could talk to about different things (school, family, feelings, hobbies)?

* Practise asking in small ways: "Can you help me with this?" "Would you sit with me while I do this?"

* Use a friend test: What would I say to a friend if they were feeling like this? Why don't I say that to myself?

* Journal prompt: What do I wish someone would offer me right now?

* Celebrate help moments: Make a "help jar" – every time you ask for support, put in a bead, note or sticker. Watch it fill up.

⭐ REFLECTION PROMPTS

1 When was the last time you really needed help but didn't ask?

2 What stopped you?

3 What might have helped you speak up?

4 Who do you feel safest asking for support? Why?

⭐ ACTIVITY: SUPPORT MAP

Draw a circle in the middle of your page and write "Me" inside it.

Create a Spider Diagram. In each one, write someone who could support you with something:

- ✧ SCHOOL STUFF
- ✧ FEELINGS
- ✧ FUN
- ✧ ADVICE
- ✧ REST

Keep the map somewhere you'll see it when things feel heavy.

⭐ FINAL MESSAGE

You don't have to do it all alone. You were never meant to.

Asking for help doesn't make you less strong. It makes you more supported. More human. More whole.

You are allowed to need things.

You are allowed to be seen.

You are allowed to be held — without apologising for it.

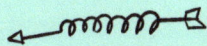

Chapter 5
When Girls Are Mean to Girls

Other girls aren't your enemy - they're your crew.

When Lucy started secondary school, she was excited.

New school, new subjects, new people.

She'd always been the kind of girl who made friends easily – bubbly, kind, quick to laugh.

So when a group of girls started chatting to her in the first few weeks, she felt lucky. They were confident. Popular. They knew how to say the right thing at the right time. Being part of their group felt like being chosen.

At first, it was fun - group selfies, inside jokes, lunchtime games.

But then the rules started to change.

One girl, Amelia, decided what music was "allowed" in the group. Another, Jade, made comments about Lucy's bag, her hair, her trainers - nothing nasty, just enough to make Lucy second-guess herself.

Sometimes they ignored her messages.

Sometimes they invited everyone else to hang out.

Sometimes they said things like, "We're just joking, don't take it so seriously."

Lucy never knew where she stood.

One day she was in. The next day, she wasn't.

She started changing small things about herself - what she wore, how she laughed, what she said in group chats. She stopped talking about the things she loved in case they were "cringe."

She tried to be what they wanted.

But it never felt like enough.

Then one lunchtime, they told her directly:

"We don't want to sit with you anymore."

Just like that.

Lucy nodded, stood up, and walked away. She didn't cry. Not then.

But inside, something cracked.

Not just because she was hurt, but because she'd tried so hard to belong.

She hadn't realised that the group she thought were her friends were really just the ones setting rules - and punishing her for not following them.

This story is for you if:

- ✶ You've changed who you are to fit into a friendship group.
- ✶ You never know where you stand with your friends.
- ✶ You've felt hurt by people you thought were your crew.

LET'S TALK ABOUT GIRL-GIRL JUDGEMENT

Here's something many of us have felt but don't talk about enough:

Sometimes, the hardest part of being a girl is the way other girls treat you.

Not all girls, and not all the time. But enough that it leaves a mark.

We're told to stick together. To support each other. But we're also raised in a culture that teaches girls to compete:

- For attention
- For popularity
- For approval
- For space
- For love

We're taught that there's not enough room for all of us. So some of us get loud, others go quiet. Some join in the jokes to feel safer. Others become the target.

> It's not because girls are mean.
> It's because we've been trained to survive systems that pit us against each other.
> This chapter is about breaking that pattern.

WHAT IS INTERNALISED MISOGYNY?

That's a big term. But here's what it means in real life:

It's when we've taken in messages about what girls should be - quiet, pretty, nice, not "too much" - and start judging other girls (and ourselves) for not fitting the mould.

It can sound like:

- "SHE'S SO FULL OF HERSELF."
- "SHE TRIES TOO HARD."
- "SHE'S TOO LOUD / TOO QUIET / TOO WEIRD / TOO BASIC."
- "AT LEAST I'M NOT LIKE HER."
- "SHE'S A 'PICK ME'".

We don't always mean to think it. But the thoughts are there, because we've grown up hearing them.

The good news? We can unlearn them. We can flip the script. We can choose something different.

WHAT IT FEELS LIKE

If you've been on the receiving end of girl-girl judgement, you might feel:

- Left out
- Picked apart
- Like you're never "just right"
- Scared to be yourself
- Afraid to trust other girls

And if you've judged another girl (even in your head), you might feel:

- Competitive
- Defensive
- Uncomfortable
- Guilty

Both sides hurt. And both are part of the same problem.

But you're not stuck in it. You're not bad. You're human, and you can absolutely do better.

WHY THIS HAPPENS

Because we're taught that:

- Girls have to be perfect to be accepted
- There's only room for one "cool" or "smart" or "funny" girl
- Being liked matters more than being real
- Being "better than" someone else keeps us safe

But these ideas divide us. They make us distrust each other. They make us lonelier.

Sisterhood isn't a trend. It's a decision. And it starts here.

DEPROGRAMMING TOOLS

* **Catch and flip:** The next time you notice a mean thought about another girl, pause. Ask: where did that come from? Then find one thing you admire instead.

* **Celebrate girls you admire:** Make a list of the girls you look up to — and why. Focus on their courage, creativity, kindness or weirdness.

* **Unpack the "mean girl" myth:** Who gets portrayed as mean or dramatic in shows, books, or TikToks? What story is being told? Who benefits from girls being divided?

* **Talk about jealousy without shame:** Jealousy is normal. But it doesn't have to turn into judgement. Say: I feel jealous AND I want to support her. Both can be true.

* **Create a Sisterhood Code:** Write your own rules for what healthy, kind, real girlhood looks like. Add to it as you grow.

⭐ REFLECTION PROMPTS

1 When have you felt judged or excluded by other girls?

2 When have you judged another girl to make yourself feel better?

3 What do you wish girls did more of for each other?

4 What kind of friendships do you want to build?

 ## ACTIVITY: SISTERHOOD CODE

On a fresh page, write the title: My Sisterhood Code

List the things you want to stand for when it comes to girls supporting girls. Here are some to get you started:

- WE DON'T TEAR EACH OTHER DOWN TO FEEL TALLER
- WE SAY NO TO GOSSIP THAT MAKES PEOPLE FEEL SMALL
- WE TALK ABOUT HARD STUFF WITHOUT BLAME
- WE LET EACH OTHER BE MESSY, REAL AND LOUD
- WE CELEBRATE WHAT MAKES EACH OTHER SHINE

Stick your Sisterhood Code in your notebook, locker or on your bedroom wall. Come back to it when things feel tricky.

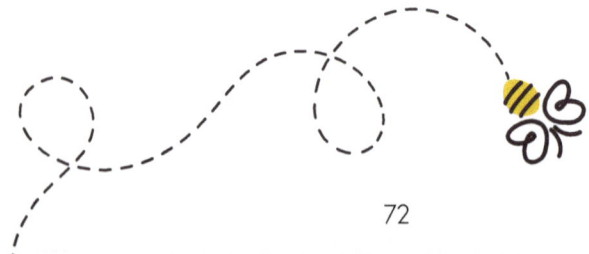

 **FINAL MESSAGE**

You don't have to compete to belong.
You don't have to shrink to stay safe.
You don't have to judge to feel powerful.
Other girls are not your enemy.
They are your mirrors. Your allies. Your teachers. Your crew.

Together, you can build something better.

Chapter 6
Is It Me or Am I Just Confused?

Learning to spot self-blame and quiet your inner critic.

"I probably said it all wrong."

Naima's heart is still thumping as she walks out of class.

She'd actually done it - she answered a question. Out loud. In front of everyone.

At the time, it felt okay. The teacher smiled. She said something about Naima making a good point. But then someone sighed. Or maybe it was just someone stretching. And someone else raised their eyebrow, or was that just how their face always looks?

Now Naima can't stop rewinding the moment.

Over and over. Picking it apart.

What if they thought she was showing off?

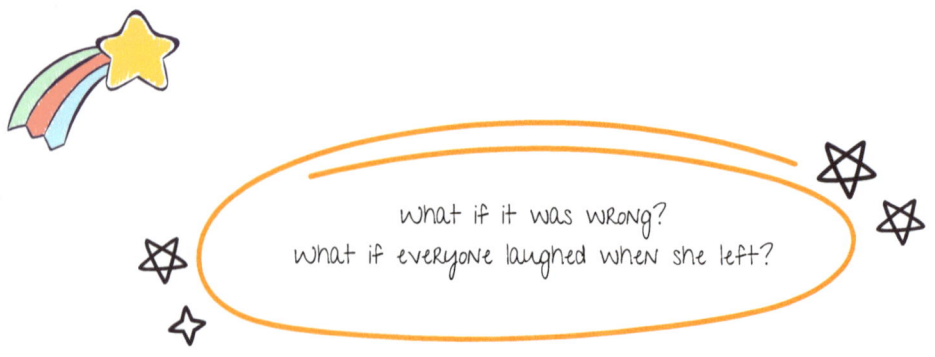

*what if it was wrong?
what if everyone laughed when she left?*

She bites the skin around her thumb and scrolls through her brain like a browser with too many tabs open.

She's not even thinking about her homework anymore.

Just about what she said. And how it sounded. And how it looked.

But later that day, as she grabs her bag to leave, a girl from her class walks past and mutters,

"That thing you said today… it actually helped. I didn't get it before."

Naima blinks. She wasn't expecting that.

The thoughts don't disappear completely, but something shifts.

Maybe… not everything she says is wrong.

Maybe… she doesn't have to be so scared of her own voice.

This story is for you if:

- ✱ You replay things you've said and question if they were "too much."
- ✱ You doubt yourself even when things go well.
- ✱ You find it hard to believe your own voice matters.

 # LET'S TALK ABOUT SELF-BLAME AND THE INNER CRITIC

Everyone has a voice in their head that offers feedback. But for many girls, that voice becomes a harsh, constant critic - especially when they try something brave or take up space.

That voice might sound like:

- ✧ "YOU'RE TOO MUCH."
- ✧ "YOU SHOULD HAVE KNOWN BETTER."
- ✧ "YOU DON'T BELONG HERE."
- ✧ "EVERYONE'S GOING TO FIGURE OUT YOU'RE FAKING IT."
- ✧ "YOU'RE NOT GOOD ENOUGH."

This voice isn't true.

It's the result of pressure, fear, and years of being trained to be perfect, pleasing and polite.

It can make you doubt your strengths. It can make you shrink. It can make you blame yourself even when nothing's gone wrong.

That voice might sound convincing, but you get to decide what's true.

 WHAT IS IMPOSTER SYNDROME?

Imposter syndrome is when you feel like a fraud, even when there's evidence you're doing well. It can show up when you:

- Get praise and feel like you didn't deserve it
- Feel pressure to be "the smart one" or "the responsible one"
- Constantly compare yourself to others
- Worry that people will "find out" you're not as good as they think

Lots of grown-ups feel this too. But it often starts early. And if we don't catch it, it sticks around for a long time.

 WHAT IT FEELS LIKE

- Doubting yourself after something good happens
- Feeling nervous when others notice your strengths
- Playing down your achievements: "It wasn't a big deal"
- Blaming yourself for tiny things
- Worrying you're not doing "enough" - even when you're trying your best

YOU'RE NOT A PROBLEM TO FIX

Let's be clear: you are not the problem. The pressure is.

The more you're told to be perfect, likeable, helpful or clever, the harder it is to feel safe making mistakes, asking questions, or just being human.

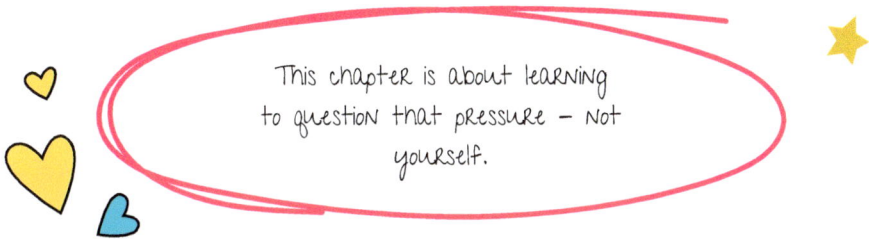

This chapter is about learning to question that pressure — not yourself.

⭐ DEPROGRAMMING TOOLS

* **Learn to name the critic:** Draw or describe your inner critic. What does it say? What does it sound like? Give it a name. (Some people call it "the Gremlin" or "the Judge.")

* **Talk back to it:** What would a kind friend say instead? Practise those phrases.

* **Spot when it shows up:** Does the voice get louder when you try something new? When you get praised? Notice its patterns.

* **Use the "what's the evidence?" test:** Ask yourself: What facts support this thought? What facts challenge it?

* **Reclaim your voice:** Write down three things you're proud of, even if they feel small. Keep adding to the list.

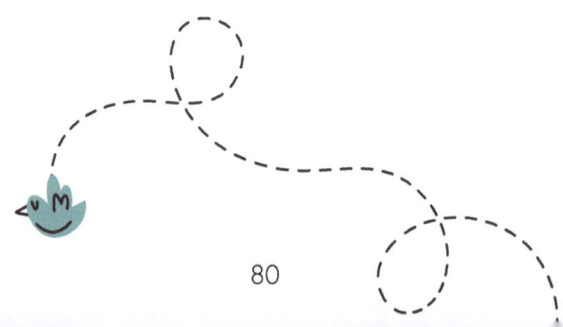

REFLECTION PROMPTS

1. What does your inner critic say to you?

2. Where do you think that voice learned those messages?

3. What would your real voice say back?

⭐ ACTIVITY: INNER CRITIC VS INNER COACH

Split your page in half.

On one side, write things your inner critic says.

On the other side, write how your inner coach (the kind, strong, real version of you) would respond.

Example:

Inner Critic	Inner Coach
YOU'RE GOING TO MESS THIS UP.	IT'S OK TO BE NERVOUS. YOU'VE HANDLED DIFFICULT TASKS BEFORE.

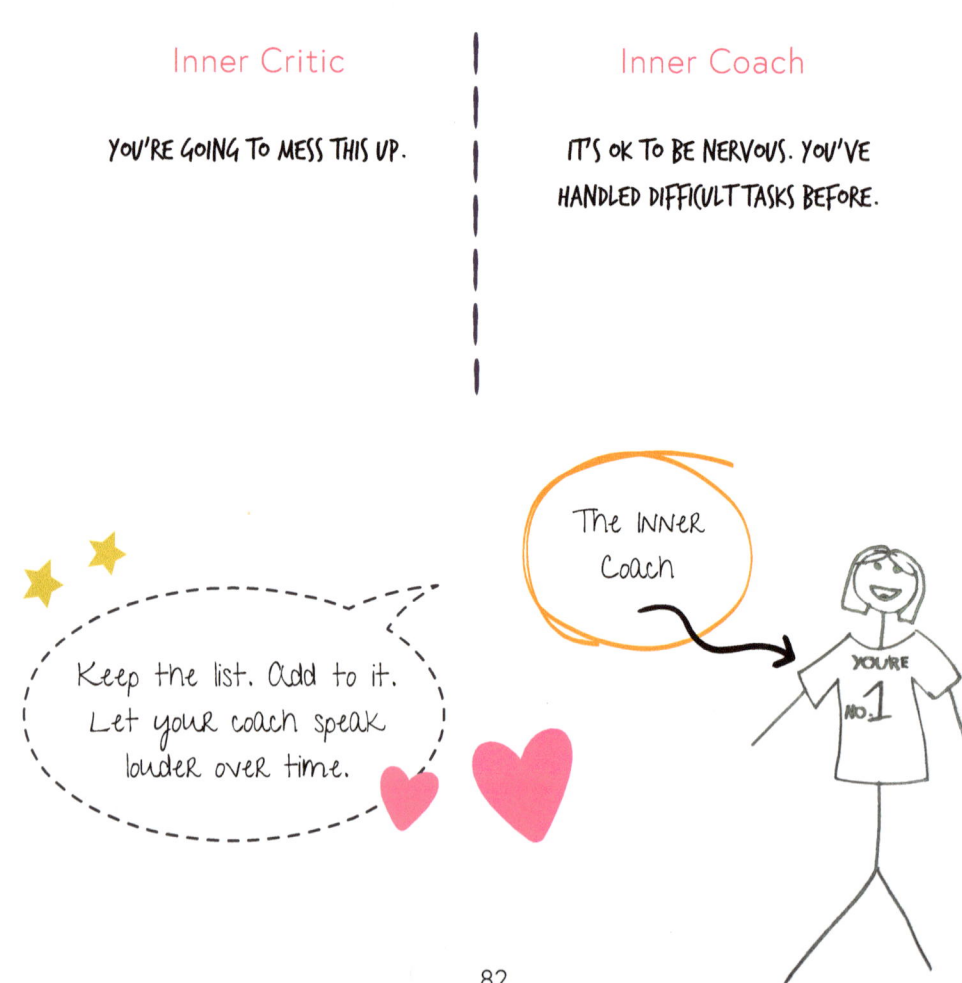

Keep the list. Add to it. Let your coach speak louder over time.

The INNER Coach

Inner Critic | Inner Coach

 FINAL MESSAGE

You don't have to be perfect to be worthy.

You don't have to be confident all the time to be capable.

You don't have to silence yourself to stay safe.

The voice that tells you you're not enough is loud — but it's not the truth.

The truth is this: You are growing. You are learning. You are already enough.

And you can trust yourself — even when your inner critic gets noisy.

Chapter 7
Tired All the Time

You are allowed to rest. It's not lazy - it's necessary.

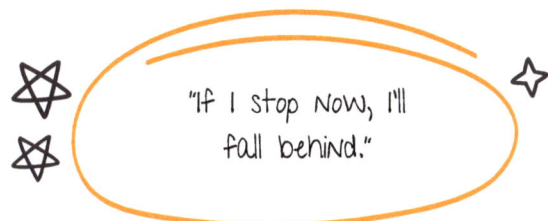

"If I stop now, I'll fall behind."

Eleni is on her third hour of revision and her brain feels like mashed potato.

The same paragraph has been staring back at her for ten minutes, but she's still highlighting it in rainbow colours like that's going to help.

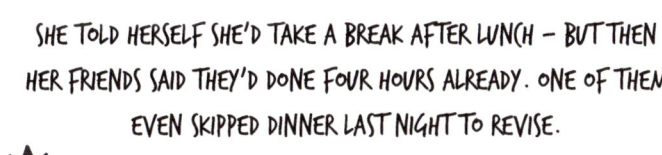

SHE TOLD HERSELF SHE'D TAKE A BREAK AFTER LUNCH – BUT THEN HER FRIENDS SAID THEY'D DONE FOUR HOURS ALREADY. ONE OF THEM EVEN SKIPPED DINNER LAST NIGHT TO REVISE.

So Eleni keeps going.

Her back aches. Her eyes burn. Her room is full of flashcards and empty mugs.

 *And she still feels like it's not enough.*

The scary part? She used to love dancing. It made her feel alive, free, happy. But she quit it this term. She said it was to focus on school - but really, she was scared.

Scared to fall behind.

Scared someone would think she wasn't trying hard enough.

Scared that if her results weren't perfect, she'd only have herself to blame.

But right now?

She's tired all the time, and her brain won't work anyway.

So the next week, she does something small but brave.

She books her old dance class. Just once.

And when she finishes, sweaty and smiling and breathless, she realises something important:

She actually feels better.

Her brain is clearer.

And she still has time to revise.

Rest isn't lazy. It's fuel.

 *And Eleni finally gets it.*

This story is for you if:

* You keep pushing yourself even when you're completely drained.
* You've stopped doing things you love to make more time for studying or work.
* You believe rest is something you have to earn.

⭐ LET'S TALK ABOUT BEING TIRED

We all get tired sometimes. But some kinds of tiredness go deeper than sleep.

Some kinds of tired come from:

- TRYING TO BE EVERYTHING FOR EVERYONE
- SAYING YES WHEN YOU MEAN NO
- ALWAYS PERFORMING, HELPING, FIXING, PLEASING
- HOLDING IN YOUR EMOTIONS
- PUSHING THROUGH WHEN YOUR BODY SAYS "REST"

That kind of tiredness isn't fixed by one early night. It's your body and mind saying:

> "I NEED A BREAK. I NEED TO FEEL SAFE. I NEED TO BREATHE."

 ## THE PRESSURE TO BE "ON"

Girls often feel like they have to:

- KEEP SMILING
- KEEP ACHIEVING
- KEEP RESPONDING
- KEEP IT ALL TOGETHER

Even when they're tired. Even when they're struggling. Even when what they really want is to stop.

This chapter is about learning that rest isn't lazy. It's not weak. It's how we recharge, reset, and come back to ourselves.

 ## WHAT BURNOUT LOOKS LIKE (EVEN IN GIRLS)

Feeling overwhelmed by small things.

Snapping at people even when you don't mean to.

Trouble concentrating.

Wanting to be alone all the time.

Crying for "no reason."

Getting headaches or tummy aches.

Feeling numb, blank, or zoned out.

These are not random. They are signs that your body is carrying more than it was built for.

YOU DON'T HAVE TO EARN REST

Rest is not something you "get" once you've achieved enough.

Rest is something you need because you are human.

And you don't have to feel guilty for it.

Even when:

- OTHER PEOPLE ARE BUSY
- YOU'RE IN THE MIDDLE OF A TO-DO LIST
- YOU DON'T HAVE A REASON TO FEEL TIRED

If your body is tired, that's reason enough.

⭐ DEPROGRAMMING TOOLS

* **Create a Rest Menu:** Make a list of things that help you feel calm, safe, and steady. Include different types: physical rest, mental rest, emotional rest, sensory rest. (Examples: lying down in silence, doodling, a warm drink, quiet music, saying no, time away from screens).

* **Track your energy:** Notice when you feel most drained during the day or week. What's happening around those times?

* **Learn the signs of burnout:** Look at your mind, mood and body. Where is tiredness showing up?

* **Challenge the "busy = better" belief:** Ask: Who told me that being busy is what makes me valuable? Is it true?

* **Say it out loud:** Practise: "I'm tired, and that's valid." You don't have to explain or apologise.

⭐ REFLECTION PROMPTS

1. What kind of tired are you right now — physical, emotional, mental, or all three?

2. When do you feel the pressure to keep going, even when you're done?

3. What does your body feel like when it's asking you to rest?

 ACTIVITY: MY REST MENU

Draw a plate (or a menu board) on a page. Split it into sections:

- QUICK BREAKS (5 – 10 MINS)
- MEDIUM REST (30 MINS – 1 HOUR)
- DEEP RECHARGE (WHEN YOU NEED REAL TIME OUT)

Fill each section with things that help you rest or reset.

Put your Rest Menu somewhere visible and choose something from it when you feel yourself running low.

 # FINAL MESSAGE

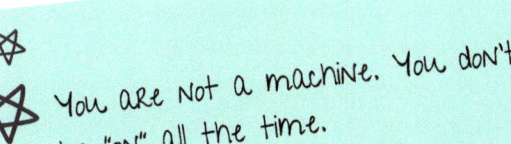

You are not a machine. You don't have to be "on" all the time.

You don't have to earn stillness. You don't have to apologise for being tired.

Rest is not a weakness. It's what helps you stay strong, clear and steady.

And it's not just allowed, it's essential.

Breathe. Pause. Begin again, when you're ready.

Chapter 8
Trying to Be Perfect

> PeRfectioN isN't the goal — being Real is.

Imogen didn't just want to do well - she wanted to do it perfectly.

Top grades. Neat handwriting. A flawless ponytail. The kind of girl who always looked like she had it together, without trying too hard.

She would never admit how much effort it really took.

The late nights. The re-doing of homework that was already "fine." The crying over a 94% instead of 100%.

No one saw that part.

Her friends thought she was confident.

Teachers praised her.

Even her parents said, "You're so lucky you don't need to stress."

But Imogen was stressed. All the time.

She once spent two hours on a piece of homework that should've taken twenty minutes. She ripped it up three times before handing it in. Not because it was wrong - but because it didn't feel perfect.

She also stopped doing things she loved, like joining the school netball team.

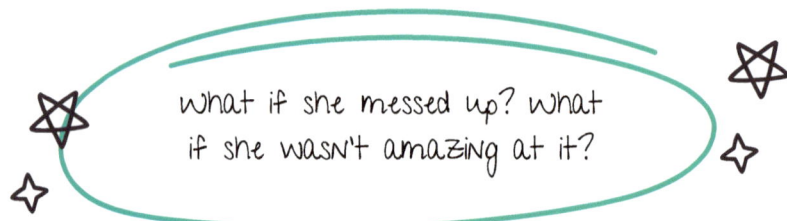

what if she messed up? what if she wasn't amazing at it?

She told herself it was a "busy term."

But really, she was scared of not being the best.

The weird thing was… even when she was the best, it didn't help.

She still felt like it wasn't enough. Like she wasn't enough.

Every time someone said,

"You're such a good girl,"

It felt less like a compliment and more like a rule she had to keep following.

Perfect wasn't just a goal anymore - it was a mask she couldn't take off.

This story is for you if:

- You aim for perfection and still feel like you're falling short.
- You hide how much effort it takes to "have it all together."
- You feel like being called a "good girl" comes with pressure, not pride.

 THE PERFECTION TRAP

Many girls grow up believing that being perfect is what makes them lovable, worthy, or safe.

Perfect at school.

Perfect at home.

Perfect in how they look, speak, behave and succeed.

And when they're not perfect?

They feel like they've failed - even if no one else thinks that.

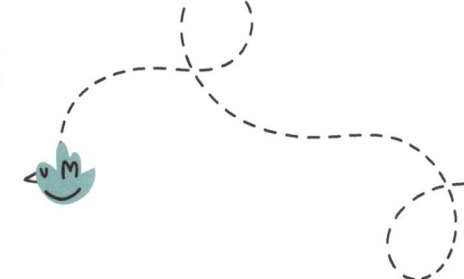

This chapter is about naming that perfection trap - and letting it go.

 WHAT IT FEELS LIKE

- Putting huge pressure on yourself to get it right every time
- Avoiding things you might not be "good at"
- Hiding your mistakes or pretending everything's fine
- Feeling proud only when you're praised
- Being scared to start unless you know you'll succeed

It's exhausting. And the truth is: perfection is a moving target. Even when you hit it, it shifts again.

 WHERE IT COMES FROM

Perfectionism often starts with praise.

- "YOU'RE SO CLEVER."
- "YOU'RE SUCH A GOOD GIRL."
- "YOU ALWAYS GET IT RIGHT."
- "YOU'RE THE RESPONSIBLE ONE."

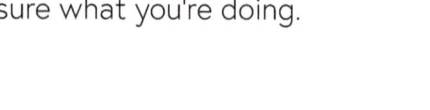

It sounds positive. But over time, it creates pressure. You feel like you always have to be the best version of yourself - even when you're tired, struggling, or not sure what you're doing.

But here's the secret: you don't have to be perfect to be powerful.

⭐ WHAT REALLY MATTERS

Mistakes matter.

Messy moments matter.

Trying and learning and falling over and getting up again — that's where growth happens.

Perfection isn't connection.

It isn't creativity.

It isn't joy.

You don't have to earn your worth by being flawless.

You are already enough.

DEPROGRAMMING TOOLS

* Make a "Proudly Imperfect" list: What are some things you did badly, failed at, or found hard — but learned something from anyway?

* Do something silly on purpose: Wear odd socks. Try a dance move and mess it up. Draw a wobbly picture. Laugh.

* Journal prompt: What would I try if I wasn't afraid of failing?

* Learn from others: Find stories of artists, athletes, writers or scientists who failed — and kept going. What helped them?

* New self-talk: Try saying: "Messy progress is better than perfect pressure." OR "Done is better than perfect."

 **REFLECTION PROMPTS**

1 What does "perfect" mean to you — and where did that idea come from?

2 When have you felt proud of yourself even when something didn't go to plan?

3 What would you like to try if being perfect wasn't part of the deal?

⭐ ACTIVITY: THE PROUDLY IMPERFECT PAGE

Draw or list things that didn't go perfectly, but still helped you grow.

They might be:
- ✧ TIMES YOU TRIED SOMETHING NEW
- ✧ MOMENTS YOU MADE A MISTAKE AND LEARNED FROM IT
- ✧ DAYS YOU RESTED INSTEAD OF PUSHING THROUGH
- ✧ ANYTHING THAT WASN'T PERFECT, BUT WAS STILL IMPORTANT

Decorate it however you like. Add to it over time. Let it be proof that imperfect is powerful.

 # FINAL MESSAGE

Perfection doesn't protect you. It just pressures you.

You don't have to be the best to be worthy. You don't have to have it all together to be loved.

You are allowed to be messy, learning, growing, and still incredible.

Let go of the pressure. Keep showing up. That's enough.

Chapter 9
Your Body Is Not the Problem

 You are an absolute miracle

> "What if we stopped trying to shrink ourselves to fit a world that was never built for us — and instead, built a new one where we all fit just as we are?"

You were never supposed to hate your body.

You were never supposed to feel shame when you looked in the mirror.

You were never supposed to waste your precious energy comparing your body to someone else's.

But somewhere along the line, you might have learned that your body is something to fix instead of something to *celebrate*. That thinner is better. That smooth is beautiful. That quiet and contained is 'feminine'. That you need to work on yourself - constantly - to be acceptable.

Here's the truth they don't want you to know:

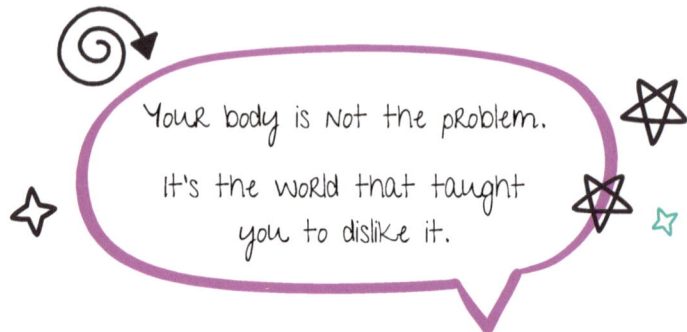

Your body is not the problem. It's the world that taught you to dislike it.

And there's *a huge amount* of money in keeping you at war with yourself.

⭐ LET'S TALK ABOUT THE BODY SHAME ECONOMY

The global beauty and wellness industry is worth *over £400 billion*. Per year. It grows bigger every year. And one of its key marketing strategies? Making women and girls feel like we're never good enough. That we need *something* - a product, a pill, a plan - to be "beautiful".

- ✧ GOT SKIN? YOU NEED FLAWLESS FOUNDATION.
- ✧ GOT CURVES? YOU NEED SHAPEWEAR.
- ✧ GOT BODY HAIR? YOU NEED RAZORS, WAX, LASERS.
- ✧ GOT FAT? YOU NEED TO LOSE IT. IMMEDIATELY.
- ✧ GOT EMOTIONS? PROBABLY HORMONES – BETTER FIX THAT TOO.

We're sold problems we didn't know we had, and then sold "solutions" to fix them.

And it's not just products - it's the entire system. Ads. Algorithms. Influencers. TV shows. Magazines. Social media filters. Even some school dress codes.

This isn't about *individual* choices - it's about a system that profits from your self-doubt.

But here's the rebellion:

You don't have to play along.

WHAT YOU SEE ISN'T ALWAYS REAL

Have you ever looked at someone online and thought:

The truth is… they probably don't.

And that's not a bad thing - it's just something you need to *know*.

Because most of what we see online - even from "normal" people - isn't real. It's:

- CAREFULLY POSED
- PERFECTLY LIT
- FILTERED OR AIRBRUSHED
- STYLED BY MAKEUP ARTISTS OR APPS
- DRESSED BY STYLISTS
- EDITED WITH PROFESSIONAL TOOLS
- OR... COMPLETELY FAKE (AI-GENERATED PEOPLE WHO DON'T EVEN EXIST)

And the scary part? Sometimes it's impossible to tell what's been changed.

 SO WHAT DOES THIS MEAN FOR YOU?

If you've ever looked at someone online and thought:

- I WISH I LOOKED LIKE THAT.
- WHY DON'T MY ARMS/STOMACH/SKIN/HAIR LOOK LIKE HERS?
- SHE'S SO EFFORTLESSLY PRETTY...

Just pause.

Breathe.

And remember: *you're comparing yourself to a highlight reel, a filter, or in some cases, a computer-generated person.* Which is so unfair.

 **REAL TALK**

Even the people in the pictures *don't look like the pictures in real life.*

They wake up with bad breath.

They get bloated.

They have stretch marks and body hair.

They get spots, dark circles and weird angles in selfies too.

They are real people - and real people aren't perfect.

 **DEPROGRAMMING TOOL: THE "SCROLL BREAK"**

When you feel that tight, twisty feeling after scrolling, try this:

1. Say out loud (or in your head): "This is not the full picture."

2. Unfollow or mute accounts that make you feel bad about yourself.

3. Follow real, diverse, joyful people instead — people who talk about feelings, fun, and real life.

And if you're feeling brave, post something real. Not polished. Not perfect. Just you.

You deserve to feel good in your skin — not because it's flawless, but because it's yours.

⭐ A DIFFERENT KIND OF ROLE MODEL: THE WOMEN'S RUGBY WORLD CUP

Let us tell you a story.

Not long ago, we sat down to watch the Women's Rugby World Cup. We expected to be impressed - and we were. But not just by the tries and tackles.

What stunned us was the *bodies*.

Muscular. Broad. Compact. Tall. Short. Fast. Powerful. Fierce. Focused.

These women weren't playing to look cute. They were playing to *win*.

And every single one of them was beautiful. Not because they fit some made-up standard of beauty - but because they were *embodied*. Inhabiting their bodies fully. Using them. Trusting them. Celebrating what they could *do*, not what they looked like.

We didn't just see athletes. We saw liberation.

It made us wonder:

> What would happen if we stopped measuring our worth by what we look like and started measuring it by what we can do, feel, create and change?

YOUR BODY'S SEASONS - UNDERSTANDING YOUR CYCLE

Your body isn't the same every day.

It changes. Cycles. Flows.

If you menstruate, you're living with a monthly rhythm that mirrors the seasons - and each one brings its own kind of energy.

Here's a simple way to understand your cycle through the four seasons:

 ### Spring (Pre-Ovulation / Follicular Phase)

- Energy rising
- Brain sharp, ideas flowing
- Great time to start new things, make plans
- You might feel lighter, more social

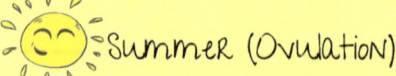 ### Summer (Ovulation)

- Peak energy, confidence boost
- Body may feel strongest
- Great time for connection, communication
- You might feel radiant, magnetic

Autumn (Post-Ovulation / Luteal Phase)

- Energy begins to slow
- More inward focus
- Great time for finishing things, reflection
- You might feel more sensitive, irritable or tired

Winter (Menstruation / Period)

- Time for rest, retreat
- Body is shedding and renewing
- Great time for reflection, intuition
- You might need more space, quiet and care

Knowing this rhythm isn't about controlling your body - it's about *understanding* it. So you can stop pushing through and start working *with* it.

Your body isn't broken.

She's just asking you to listen.

⭐ DEPROGRAMMING LIES ABOUT YOUR BODY

Let's break down some common messages you've probably absorbed - and replace them with the truth.

The Lie	The Truth
You have to be skinny to be beautiful.	Beauty has *no* size. Health and worth come in every shape.
Your body is for other people to look at.	Your body is *yours*. For living, moving, dancing, resting, *being*.
Body hair is gross.	Body hair is natural. Removing it is a choice - not an obligation.
You should always be confident.	Some days are hard. Confidence grows when we *honour* ourselves, not ignore how we feel.
If you don't love your body, you're failing.	Some days "I accept my body" is powerful. You don't need to perform confidence.

DEPROGRAMMING TOOLS

The Mirror Reframe

When you look in the mirror, don't start with judgement. Try asking:

* What has this body done for me today?
* How can I say thank you to her?

Unfollow to Heal

Clear out your feed. Follow people with diverse bodies, voices, lives. Representation matters.

Body Story Collage

Create a collage (digital or physical) about your body story: what it's done, what it's survived, how it's grown. Include photos, drawings, quotes, or poetry.

Cycle Tracker

Use a journal or app to track your physical and emotional rhythms. Note energy, mood, pain, cravings, motivation. Watch your own patterns.

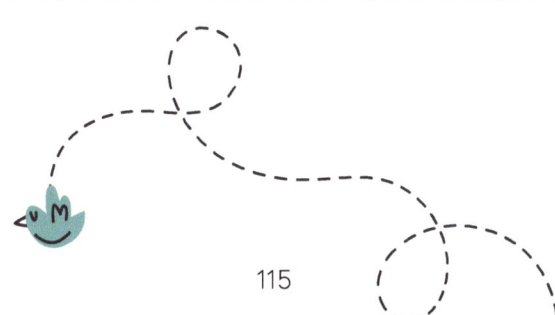

⭐ REFLECTION PROMPTS

1 What is one thing your body lets you do that you're proud of?

2 When do you feel most connected to your body?

3 What messages have you absorbed about how girls should look — and do you agree?

4 What would it feel like to trust your body more?

ACTIVITY: WRITE A LETTER TO YOUR BODY

Start with:

> "DEAR BODY,
>
> I'M SORRY FOR...
>
> I'M GRATEFUL FOR...
>
> I WANT TO...
>
> LOVE, ME"

This can be private. But if it feels powerful, read it aloud to yourself in the mirror. You might be surprised at what comes up.

⭐ FINAL WORDS

Your body is not a mistake.

It's not a project.

It's not a before-and-after photo.

It is your home.

Your instrument.

Your constant companion.

There is no 'right' way to have a girl's body.

There is only your way.

You don't have to earn your worth by shrinking, straightening, smoothing or silencing your body.

You already have it.

You are whole.

You are worthy.

Exactly as you are.

Chapter 10
The Should Monster

Not every rule is right for you.

Tara sat on her bedroom floor, staring at the pile of clothes in front of her.

She was packing for her first school residential - two nights away, sharing a room with three girls from her form. It should have been exciting. But instead, it felt like a test she didn't know how to pass.

She picked up her favourite fluffy pyjamas.

They were soft. Cosy. Safe.

But suddenly, they looked childish.

Should I take something cooler?

Do people wear those silky matching ones now?

What if I look like I'm trying too hard? What if I don't try hard enough?

Every item brought another question.

Trainers - Should they be the "right" brand?

Snacks - Should she bring enough to share? Or was that try-hard too?

Phone case - Was it too babyish? Should she switch it out?

Even her pillow - Should she pretend she didn't bring one? Would that seem more chill?

She wasn't even there yet, but she already felt like she was getting it wrong.

She told her mum she was "just tired," but really, her brain was full of rules she couldn't remember learning - rules about fitting in, about being liked, about not being too loud, too quiet, too much, or too different.

She wanted to be herself.

But right now, she didn't even know who that was - just who she should be.

So she folded up the fluffy pyjamas.

And packed the ones she didn't like as much.

This story is for you if:

✱ You second-guess every choice in case it's "wrong."

✱ You feel like you're constantly trying to fit in without knowing the rules.

✱ You worry more about being acceptable than being yourself.

⭐ THE "SHOULD" VOICE

Have you ever heard a voice in your head saying what you should do?

"I SHOULD BE QUIETER."

"I SHOULD ALREADY KNOW HOW TO DO THIS."

"I SHOULD BE NICER, SMARTER, BETTER, LESS EMOTIONAL..."

"I SHOULD GO ALONG WITH IT TO AVOID DRAMA."

"I SHOULD KEEP PEOPLE HAPPY."

The Should Monster

That voice can sound like your own - but often, it's made up of things you've picked up from other people: family, school, social media, books, teachers, even friends.

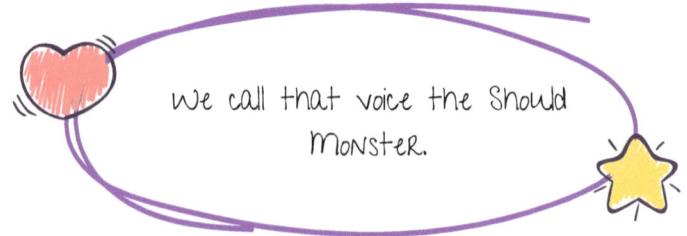

We call that voice the Should Monster.

It's not evil. It's not trying to hurt you. But it is trying to control you, quietly and constantly.

⭐ WHERE THE "SHOULDS" COME FROM

Some shoulds are useful:

- "I SHOULD BRUSH MY TEETH."
- "I SHOULD TREAT PEOPLE WITH RESPECT."

But many shoulds are about fitting in, not being well. They come from:

- GENDER RULES
- CULTURAL EXPECTATIONS
- FEAR OF JUDGEMENT
- TRYING TO PLEASE EVERYONE

They're not about you. They're about keeping you small, quiet or safe according to someone else's rules.

⭐ WHAT IT FEELS LIKE

If you're living under too many "shoulds", you might feel:

- ✧ STRESSED AND UNSURE
- ✧ LIKE YOU'RE NEVER DOING ENOUGH
- ✧ DISCONNECTED FROM WHAT YOU WANT
- ✧ GUILTY FOR DISAPPOINTING OTHERS
- ✧ LIKE YOUR VOICE IS BURIED UNDER OTHER PEOPLE'S EXPECTATIONS

You might not even know what your real choices are anymore.

⭐ THE GOOD NEWS

You don't have to obey every "should". You can pause. Ask where it came from. Decide whether it actually fits you.

You get to rewrite the rules.

DEPROGRAMMING TOOLS

* **Write down your top "shoulds":** List the ones that come up often. Then ask: who told me this? Do I agree? Does it help or hurt me?

* **Try saying "According to who?":** When a new rule pops up (on social media, in a conversation, in your head), challenge it. According to who? is a powerful question.

* **Create a "Could / Should / Want" triangle:** When making a decision, write:
  - What could I do? (All the options)
  - What do I feel I should do? (External pressure)
  - What do I actually want to do? (Your real voice)

* **Make a personal values list:** What do you care about? Kindness? Creativity? Justice? Curiosity? When your decisions come from your values, not your fears, you feel more free.

* **Draw your Should Monster:** What does it look like? What does it say? What are its favourite rules? Then write new rules beside it — ones that serve you.

REFLECTION PROMPTS

1 What's a "should" you've believed for a long time — but now want to question?

2 Where do most of your shoulds come from — family, school, friends, online?

3 What's one thing you've done recently because you wanted to, not because you "should"?

 ACTIVITY: DRAW AND RENAME YOUR SHOULD MONSTER

Give your Should Monster a face. A name. A catchphrase.

Then rewrite its rulebook.

Instead of:

"YOU SHOULD KEEP QUIET TO BE LIKED."

Try:

"YOU CAN SPEAK UP WITH KINDNESS AND STILL BE RESPECTED."

Instead of:

"YOU SHOULD SAY YES SO NO ONE'S UPSET."

Try:

"YOU CAN SAY NO AND STILL BE A GOOD FRIEND."

Keep your new rulebook somewhere visible.

 # FINAL MESSAGE

"Should" is a word that sounds like safety, but sometimes, it's just fear in disguise.

You don't have to live by rules that shrink you.

You are allowed to ask: According to who?

You are allowed to choose what fits, and leave the rest behind.

Your voice matters. Your wants matter. Your values matter.

The Should Monster doesn't get the final say. You do.

Chapter 11
Please Like Me!

You don't need permission to be yourself.

Anaya used to feel like she knew who she was.

She liked bold earrings, big opinions, and writing stories with strange characters and twist endings.

Her Year 6 teacher had called her "brave" for how confidently she spoke up.

She believed it.

But starting her new school in Year 7 was like walking into a room where all the lights had dimmed.

Everyone already seemed to know the rules - what to wear, what to post, what to laugh at and what not to say out loud.

So Anaya adjusted.

She nodded when she didn't agree.

She laughed when jokes made her uncomfortable.

She changed how she spoke, just a little, and swapped out her favourite things for whatever was "cool" that week.

People liked her.

She got invited to things.

She wasn't left out.

But she also wasn't sure who they actually liked - them, or the version of herself she was carefully editing every day.

At home, she was exhausted.

Always thinking about what to post, what to wear, how to reply to the group chat without sounding "cringe."

She found herself hesitating before she said anything - even around her real friends.

Because the scariest thought in her head was:

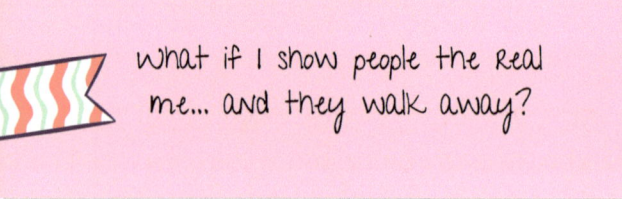

What if I show people the real me... and they walk away?

So instead, she stayed likeable.

And quiet.

And slowly, quietly, a little bit lost.

This story is for you if:

* You've started hiding parts of yourself to fit in.
* You worry that being truly yourself might push people away.
* You feel liked – but not truly seen.

⭐ LET'S TALK ABOUT WANTING TO BE LIKED

There's nothing wrong with wanting to be liked. It's human.

We all want to feel seen, included, and understood.

But when wanting to be liked turns into needing to be liked, it gets hard to know where others end and you begin.

You might:

- Say yes when you want to say no
- Change how you dress or act to fit in
- Overthink what people think of you
- Post things online for likes, not because they matter to you
- Feel panicked if someone's annoyed, even when you've done nothing wrong

This is called people-pleasing. And it's not your fault.

Girls are often raised to believe that being liked is more important than being real.

This chapter is about changing that belief.

 WHAT IT FEELS LIKE

When you're caught in the approval trap, you might feel:

- Exhausted from managing how others see you
- Fake or disconnected from your real self
- Constantly on edge, trying to keep everyone happy
- Unsure whether your choices are actually yours

It can feel like you're performing a version of yourself to stay liked. And it's tiring.

 YOU'RE ALLOWED TO LIKE YOURSELF FIRST

Here's something powerful:

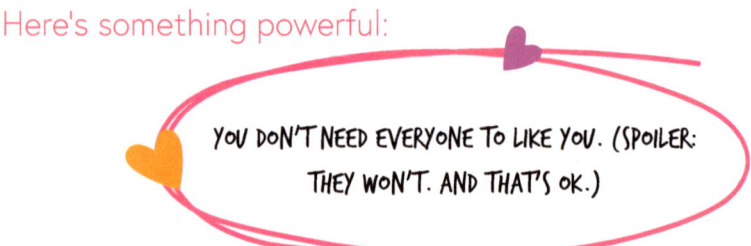

YOU DON'T NEED EVERYONE TO LIKE YOU. (SPOILER: THEY WON'T. AND THAT'S OK.)

What matters more is whether you like you.

Not in a "perfect all the time" way, but in a deep, gentle, honest way.

The kind that says:

"I KNOW WHO I AM."

"I KNOW WHAT MATTERS TO ME."

"I DON'T NEED PERMISSION TO BE MYSELF."

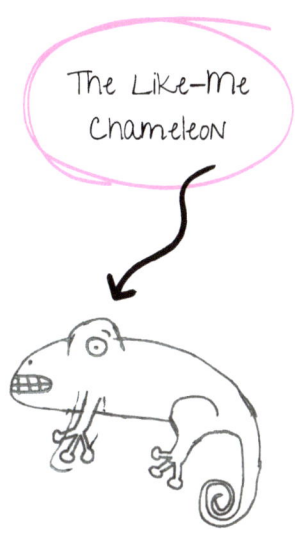

The Like-Me Chameleon

MAKING SENSE OF FEEDBACK

Just because someone says it, doesn't mean it's true.

When someone gives you feedback, whether it's a compliment, a criticism, or a throwaway comment, it can be hard to know what to do with it.

You might feel:

- Excited (they noticed me!)
- Embarrassed (why are they looking at me?)
- Confused (is that kind or shady?)
- Hurt (I didn't ask for that…)
- Unsure (should I change something about myself now?)

Here's something to remember:

> **FEEDBACK USUALLY TELLS YOU MORE ABOUT THE PERSON GIVING IT THAN IT DOES ABOUT YOU.**

It often reflects:

- Their preferences
- Their mood
- Their beliefs
- What they value
- What they were taught is "good", "clever", "polite", "feminine", etc.

That doesn't mean all feedback is bad. But it does mean you get to pause before you believe it.

 QUESTIONS TO ASK YOURSELF

When you get feedback (or compliments or comments), try asking:

1. Is it true? Does it fit with what I know about myself?
2. Is it fair? Was it said with kindness, or control?
3. Is it useful? Can I learn something from it?
4. Is it mine to carry? Or is it someone else's expectation?

If the answer is no, you can always say (even in your head):

"Thanks, but that doesn't fit me."

A NOTE ON ADULTS

Sometimes feedback comes from teachers, coaches or adults you respect. That can feel extra hard to question.

You might hear:

> "I'M JUST TRYING TO HELP."
>
> "THIS IS FOR YOUR OWN GOOD."
>
> "YOU'RE TOO SENSITIVE."
>
> "I EXPECTED MORE FROM YOU."

It's OK to feel uncomfortable.

You can take what's useful, and leave what's not.

Even adults get it wrong sometimes. That doesn't make you wrong.

TRY SAYING (OR THINKING)...

> "THAT'S ONE WAY TO SEE IT, I SEE IT DIFFERENTLY."
>
> "THANKS, I'LL THINK ABOUT THAT."
>
> "THAT'S THEIR OPINION. IT DOESN'T HAVE TO BECOME MY TRUTH."
>
> "THAT DIDN'T FEEL FAIR. I'LL TALK TO SOMEONE I TRUST ABOUT IT."

DEPROGRAMMING TOOLS

* **Make a "What I Like About Myself" card:** Write things you value about who you are (not just what you do). Revisit it often.

* **Pause before posting:** Ask: "Am I doing this for me, or for someone else's reaction?"

* **Start a "Validation Jar":** Each time you say something kind to yourself, write it down and drop it in. Watch it grow.

* **Explore compliments:** Which ones feel real? Which ones feel icky or fake? Why?

* **Practise a small no:** Say no to something small, a message, an activity, a favour, and notice what it feels like to honour yourself.

⭐ REFLECTION PROMPTS

1 When do you feel most like your real self?

2 What kind of compliments feel meaningful to you – and why?

3 What scares you most about someone not liking you?

4 What would you do differently if you trusted your own opinion more?

ACTIVITY: "WHAT I LIKE ABOUT ME" CARD

Create a mini card or poster. Write or draw five things you like about yourself - not just what you're good at, but who you are.

Examples:

I'M HONEST.

I CARE DEEPLY.

I'M CURIOUS.

I STAND UP FOR OTHERS.

I'M LEARNING TO BE MORE MYSELF.

Decorate it. Keep it somewhere special. Look at it when the "Please like me!" voice gets loud.

 **FINAL MESSAGE**

You are not here to be liked by everyone.
You are here to become you.
You don't need to shrink to be accepted.
You don't need permission to take up space.
You don't need approval to be enough.
Some people will get you. Some won't. That's life.
What matters most is that you get you.
And you like who you're becoming.

That's where the real magic lives.

Chapter 12
Not Feeling Strong

You have power – even when you feel small.

Soraya never felt like the brave one.

She wasn't the loudest in class.

She didn't raise her hand unless she really knew the answer.

She didn't run for school council or speak in assemblies.

She mostly stayed quiet - and safe.

But she felt things deeply.

She worried a lot. About her exams. About what people thought of her. About whether she was ever going to feel proud of herself.

Her cousin seemed to have it all - confident, clever, funny, easy-going. Soraya felt… small next to him.

And it didn't help that when she tried to play hockey (the sport her dad loved), she held back. She never quite went for it. And when her dad walked away from one of her matches, shaking his head, she felt like she'd failed completely.

But here's what no one saw:

SORAYA KEPT TRYING.

EVEN WHEN IT WAS HARD.

EVEN WHEN SHE WAS SCARED.

EVEN WHEN NO ONE CLAPPED OR NOTICED.

That is strength. Quiet, steady strength.

This chapter is for anyone who thinks being strong means being loud or fearless.

Sometimes the strongest people are the ones who keep going - even when it feels like no one sees them.

This story is for you if:

* You don't see yourself as brave, even though you keep going.

* You compare yourself to others and feel like you come up short.

* You underestimate the strength it takes to try – especially when no one notices.

LET'S TALK ABOUT NOT FEELING STRONG

Sometimes, strength looks loud.

Like speeches, protests, marching on stage.

But sometimes, it's quiet.

It's the tiny moment you almost give in - but don't.

It's asking a question, even when your voice shakes.

It's choosing what's right for you, even when it's awkward.

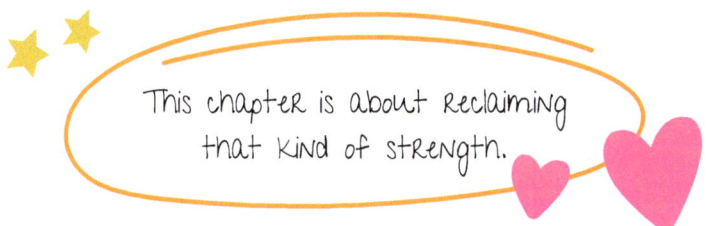

This chapter is about reclaiming that kind of strength.

WHEN YOU DON'T FEEL LIKE YOU HAVE A SAY

You might:

- Stay silent, even when you have something important to say.
- Think "it won't make a difference".
- Go along with decisions, even when you don't agree.
- Feel like your voice doesn't matter - or won't be taken seriously.
- Feel frustrated or invisible, but not know how to change it.

If any of this feels familiar: you're not broken. You're not weak.

You've probably just been taught - directly or indirectly - that your power isn't welcome.

Now it's time to unlearn that.

YOU STILL HAVE POWER

Even when you feel unsure.

Even when you're the youngest, the quietest, the least experienced.

You still have:

* a voice
* a choice
* a perspective that matters

Power doesn't mean having all the answers. It means knowing you get to take up space - even when you're still figuring things out.

DEPROGRAMMING TOOLS

- **Role-play speaking up:** Practise using your voice in fun, low-pressure ways. For example:

  "Excuse me, I'd like the last biscuit."

  "Actually, I disagree. Pineapple does belong on pizza."

  Build your confidence in safe spaces first.

- **Create a "Power Circle":** Draw a circle. Inside, list what you can control (your voice, your choices, your reactions). Outside, list what you can't. Focus your energy on the inside.

- **Learn about girls who used their voices:** Research young activists, writers, artists or leaders who made change. What helped them speak up?

- **Set a Tiny Brave Goal:** Each week, try one small brave thing.

  Say no. Ask a question. Share your opinion.

  It doesn't have to be big — it just has to be yours.

- **Use an affirmation:**

  "My voice matters."

  Say it in the mirror. Whisper it in your head. Write it on a sticky note. Remind yourself.

REFLECTION PROMPTS

1 When have you stayed quiet – even when you wanted to speak?

2 What stops you from using your voice sometimes?

3 What would change if you believed your words were worth hearing?

 ACTIVITY: POWER CIRCLE

On a blank page, draw two circles - one inside the other, like a doughnut. See next page.

In the middle circle, write the things you can control:

{
- YOUR TONE
- HOW YOU SPEAK UP
- WHO YOU TRUST
- WHAT YOU STAND FOR
- YOUR ATTITUDE
}

In the outer circle, write the things you can't control:

{
- OTHER PEOPLE'S REACTIONS
- WHO LISTENS
- WHO AGREES
- WHETHER SOMEONE INTERRUPTS
}

> Let this be your Reminder:
> You don't have to control everything to make an impact.
> You just have to own what's yours.

⭐ FINAL MESSAGE

You won't always feel strong. That's normal.

But your strength doesn't disappear just because you can't feel it.

It's there – in the choice to try.

In the quiet no.

In the "I'm not sure, but I want to find out."

In every time you stay true to yourself, even when it's hard.

Your voice matters. Your choices matter.

You don't need permission to take up space.

You already have it.

Chapter 13
Feeling Worried All the Time

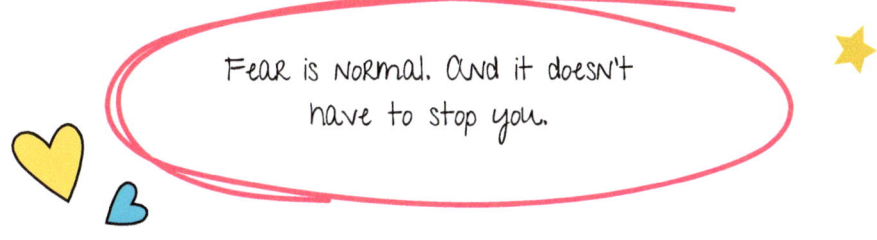

Fear is normal. And it doesn't have to stop you.

Layla had always been a worrier.

She worried at night about her parents getting into a car crash, or her little brother falling down the stairs, or her dog running away and never coming back.

She knew it didn't make sense.

She knew worrying wouldn't stop bad things from happening.

But knowing that didn't help.

Her mum once told her that worrying thoughts were like tomato plants - the more you fed them, the bigger they grew.

And Layla believed her.

But she still couldn't stop watering them.

So when she walked into her geography classroom and remembered - too late - that there was a test she'd completely forgotten to revise for, her brain didn't just go into stress mode.

It went into overdrive.
Her heart started racing.
Her hands felt weird and tingly.
Her chest got tight, and her mind went blank, like someone had suddenly wiped away everything she'd ever learned.

She kept her head down, pretending to work, but she wasn't answering anything.

She just sat there, panicking silently.

No one noticed. No one helped.

And when the bell rang, she left the room with her heart still hammering and her legs shaking.

After that, the fear didn't go away.

She was scared it might happen again - in maths, in science, in any lesson where she might be put on the spot.

So she started holding herself back.

She didn't raise her hand.

She didn't push herself.

And sometimes, she didn't even try.

Not because she didn't care.

But because she did - so much - and the thought of freezing again was too much to bear.

This story is for you if:

- ✸ You worry so much it stops you from doing the things you want to do.

- ✸ Anxiety shows up in your body, not just your thoughts.

- ✸ You've started holding back — not because you don't care, but because you're scared to fail.

⭐ LET'S TALK ABOUT FEAR

Everyone feels scared sometimes.

That's your brain doing its job: trying to keep you safe.

But sometimes your brain gets it wrong.

It reacts to new things, big feelings or tiny risks as if they're dangerous - even when they're not.

That's when fear gets loud. Bossy. Dramatic.

And if we're not careful, it starts making the decisions.

This chapter is about learning to listen to fear - but not obey it.

⭐ WHAT IT FEELS LIKE

A RACING HEART

A SHAKY OR SICK FEELING IN YOUR TUMMY

WORRY THOUGHTS THAT GO ROUND AND ROUND

A FEELING THAT SOMETHING BAD IS GOING TO HAPPEN

AVOIDING THINGS, EVEN IF YOU REALLY WANT TO TRY

Anxiety isn't just fear, it's fear that sticks around and builds stories in your head:

If I mess up, everything will fall apart.

Everyone will laugh at me.

I can't handle it.

But you can handle it.

You just need to remember how.

⭐ COURAGE ISN'T THE ABSENCE OF FEAR

> Courage isn't about not being scared. It's about feeling scared, and choosing to show up anyway.
> You don't need to be fearless. You just need to take one brave step at a time.

DEPROGRAMMING TOOLS

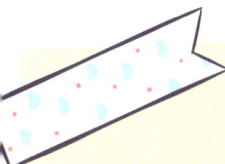

* **Create a "Fear Ladder":** Pick something that feels scary. Break it into tiny steps. Start with the easiest, then go one rung higher each time. (Example: Speak in front of one friend – Record a voice note – Say something in class.)

* **Talk back to fear like a character:** Imagine fear as a loud sidekick. You can say: "Thanks for trying to protect me, Fear – but I've got this."

* **Track your courage:** Keep a list (or chart or journal) of things that felt scary – but you did them anyway. Even small things count.

* **Practise grounding or breathing tools:** Try box breathing (in for 4, hold for 4, out for 4, hold for 4). Or use your senses: What can I see? Hear? Feel? Smell? Taste?

* **Make a Courage Jar:** Every time you do something brave (big or tiny), add a bead, pebble or folded note. Watch your courage grow over time.

⭐ REFLECTION PROMPTS

1 What is fear trying to protect you from right now?

2 What's something small you'd try if you weren't so worried about getting it wrong?

3 When have you felt scared — but done something brave anyway?

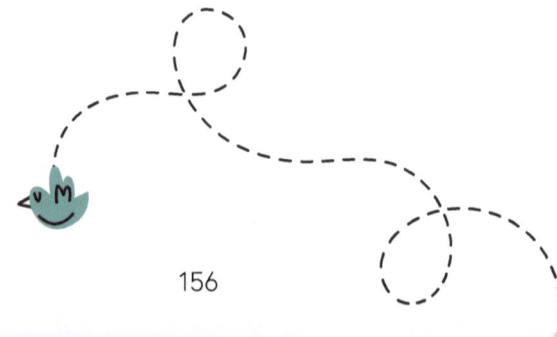

 ## ACTIVITY: MEET YOUR FEAR VOICE

Draw your fear like a character. Give it a name, a style, a personality.

Does it shout or whisper? Is it silly, serious or sneaky?

Then write a message back from your courage voice.

What does it want you to know?

Example:

> FEAR: "DON'T SPEAK, YOU'LL SOUND WEIRD."
>
> COURAGE: "EVEN IF MY VOICE SHAKES, I HAVE SOMETHING TO SAY."

Keep this page and revisit it when fear gets loud.

⭐ FINAL MESSAGE

You don't have to get rid of fear to move forward.

You just have to stop letting it be in charge.

You are allowed to feel shaky and still be brave.

You are allowed to mess up and try again.

You are allowed to be afraid — and still show up anyway.

Every act of courage — tiny or huge — rewrites the story fear is trying to tell.

> You've got this.
>
> And your courage? It's already growing.

Chapter 14
Am I Ever Good Enough?

You are already enough — no proving required.

Eesha ticked all the boxes.

She got good grades.

She showed up on time.

She was polite to teachers, helpful at home, and responsible with her little brother.

People said things like, "You've got so much potential."

They said she was hardworking, sensible, sorted.

And she was.

Except for the part where she didn't believe any of it.

Because inside, Eesha never felt like she was quite enough.

She couldn't relax unless everything was done - and even then, she'd find something else to fix or improve.

She never let herself celebrate doing well, because she thought she could've done better.

She brushed off compliments. "It was just luck."

She compared herself to everyone, all the time, even people she didn't like, even people who weren't trying.

And no matter how much she achieved, there was always a voice in her head whispering,

TRY HARDER.

BE MORE.

DON'T LET ANYONE DOWN.

When she talked about the future, her voice got quieter.

Because what she wanted, really wanted, was to go to art school.

To spend her life creating, designing, making something beautiful.

But that didn't seem good enough.

Not for her family.

Not for the people who had always expected her to be something "better."

Not for the version of herself she felt she had to live up to.

So she smiled.

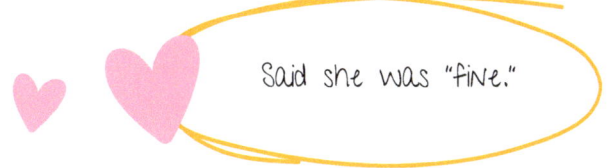

And quietly carried the weight of never feeling like she was allowed to just be who she was - without earning it.

This story is for you if:

* You achieve a lot but still feel like it's never enough.

* You dismiss compliments and downplay your success.

* You feel pressure to be someone else's version of "successful" instead of your own.

⭐ LET'S TALK ABOUT WORTH

It's easy to think your worth is something you have to earn.

> THROUGH GOOD GRADES.
>
> THROUGH BEING LIKED.
>
> THROUGH LOOKING RIGHT, ACTING RIGHT, SAYING THE RIGHT THING AT THE RIGHT TIME.

But here's the truth:

You were enough the day you were born. You're still enough now. And you'll be enough tomorrow, even if you mess up.

You don't need to be perfect to be worthy.

You don't need to be impressive to matter.

You don't need to perform to be loved.

⭐ WHEN YOU FEEL "NOT ENOUGH"

You might:

- Compare yourself constantly
- Downplay your achievements
- Feel like others are better, smarter, prettier, funnier, more
- Say "I'm fine" when you're not, because you don't want to be a bother
- Think: If I just do a bit more, then maybe I'll feel OK

> This chapter is about realising you don't need to do more to deserve love, rest, or respect. You just need to come home to yourself.

SELF-WORTH VS SELF-ESTEEM

Self-esteem is how you feel about yourself on a good day. It can go up and down.

Self-worth is deeper. It says:

- "EVEN WHEN I FEEL LOW, I STILL MATTER."
- "EVEN WHEN I MESS UP, I STILL BELONG."
- "EVEN WHEN I'M NOT CHOSEN, I'M STILL ENOUGH."

You don't have to feel amazing every day to know that you are worthy.

You just have to remember that your value isn't up for debate.

 **DEPROGRAMMING TOOLS**

* **Daily "I am..." affirmations:** Make them silly, serious, strong or soft.

    "I am thoughtful."
    "I am enough, even when I'm tired."
    "I am weird and wonderful."
    "I am still learning — and that's OK."

* **Create a collage:** Fill a page with pictures, words, colours and quotes that reflect your real self—strengths, passions, weirdness, softness. Let it be messy. Let it be you.

* **Write a love letter to your younger self:** What do you wish someone had told you when you were smaller? Now, write it to that version of you — from who you are today.

* **Unfollow accounts that make you feel less-than:** Your feed should feed you — not make you feel like you have to shrink or chase perfection.

* **Repeat this to yourself often:** "I don't have to do, to deserve. I already matter."

⭐ REFLECTION PROMPTS

1 What do you think "being enough" means — and who taught you that?

2 When do you feel most at peace with yourself?

3 What would you say to a friend who felt like they weren't enough? Can you say it to yourself too?

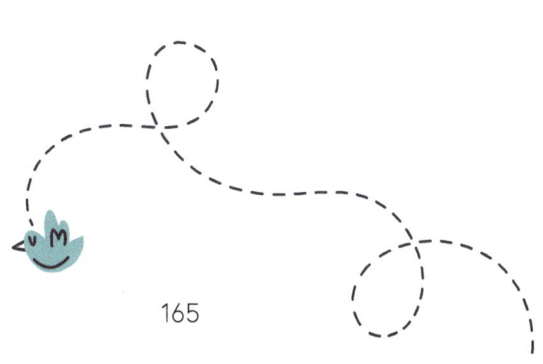

 ACTIVITY: THE "ENOUGH" WALL

Make a list, drawing or poster with the title: "I Am Already Enough Because…"

Write things that have nothing to do with achievement.

Examples:

- I TRY AGAIN WHEN THINGS ARE HARD
- I CARE ABOUT PEOPLE
- I NOTICE LITTLE THINGS
- I'M STILL HERE
- I BREATHE, I EXIST, I BELONG

Decorate it however you want. Put it somewhere you can see it often.

Let it remind you: you are not a project to fix. You are already whole.

⭐ FINAL MESSAGE

You don't have to wait to be thinner, cleverer, more confident or more "together" to be worthy.

You already are.

Right now. As you are. With all your mess, your magic, your questions, and your courage.

You are not behind. You are not broken. You are not less-than.

You are enough. You always have been.

And you always will be.

Chapter 15
Safety & Consent Toolkit

"You are the boss of your body, your choices, and your space."

Ava had just turned 12 when she got her first group invite to a "Snapchat birthday sleepover." It sounded fun - snacks, TikToks, even make-your-own bubble tea. But something felt weird when a girl she barely knew whispered, "We're gonna play a spicy game later. You in?"

Ava laughed politely. But her stomach went tight.

What kind of game? Why whisper? Do I have to?

Later that night, a message pinged:

 "SEND A PIC – IT'S JUST FOR US."

Ava stared at it. She felt frozen. Her brain went a bit foggy.

She didn't want to seem boring. Or babyish. Or dramatic.

But she also didn't want to send a photo.

So she didn't.

Instead, she typed:

"HEY – NOT REALLY MY THING. I'M GONNA SIT THIS ONE OUT."

Then she took a deep breath, blocked the sender, and told her older cousin what happened.

And you know what? Nothing exploded. No one shouted. Her cousin gave her a hug, and said, "You listened to yourself. That's called trusting your gut."

This story is for you if:

* You've ever felt pressure to join in with something that didn't feel right.

* You worry about seeming "boring" or "babyish" for setting boundaries.

* You're learning to trust your gut – even when it's uncomfortable.

REAL TALK: WHAT IS CONSENT?

Consent means saying YES freely, clearly, and comfortably.

It means:

- You want to.
- You feel safe.
- You're not being pushed, guilted, dared, or scared into it.

You can say NO - even if:

- You said yes before.
- They're your friend.
- It's "just a joke".
- You're worried they'll get mad.

Your body and your time are yours. Always.

 ## YOUR SAFETY SIGNALS

Sometimes your body tells you when something isn't OK - even before your brain works it out. These feelings are your safety radar.

Have you ever felt:

- A weird knot in your stomach?
- Like your heart's pounding too fast?
- A bit frozen, like you can't speak?
- A strong "Ugh" or "I don't like this" feeling?

That's your body saying: "Something's off."

Listen to it. It's never wrong.

 ## SAFE WAYS TO SAY NO

You are allowed to say no. Here are some words to help:

"I DON'T WANT TO."

"THAT'S NOT FOR ME."

"I'M NOT OK WITH THIS."

"PLEASE STOP."

"I NEED TO TALK TO SOMEONE FIRST."

And guess what? "No." is a full sentence. You don't have to explain.

 ONLINE CONSENT: BIG ENERGY

If someone sends you a message that makes you feel weird, embarrassed, or nervous - it's not your fault. And you are not alone.

You never have to:

- Send a photo of your body
- Join a game or challenge you're not OK with
- Stay in a chat that feels gross, mean or unsafe

What to do:

- Block the person.
- Tell an adult you trust (even if you're scared).
- Breathe - you are not in trouble.

 **WHO ARE YOUR TRUSTED ADULTS?**

Let's make a Support Map together.

Write down 3–5 people you could talk to if you felt worried or unsafe:

* a parent or carer
* a teacher
* a school counsellor or nurse
* a friend's older sibling
* a club leader
* a relative
* a friend's parent

Now circle the one you feel safest starting with.

THE "WHAT IF?" GAME

Let's practise your power.

What would you do if...

1. Someone asks you to keep a secret that feels wrong?
2. A friend dares you to send a photo "just for fun"?
3. A grown-up makes a comment that makes you feel uncomfortable?
4. Someone tells you you'll be "boring" if you don't join in?

Write down your answers. Then say them out loud. Practising makes it easier when it's real.

ACTIVITY: WHAT MAKES ME FEEL SAFE?

Draw or list 5 things, places or people that make you feel:

- ✳ Safe
- ✳ Calm
- ✳ Strong
- ✳ Brave

Put your picture on your wall, notebook or phone. Let it remind you of your power.

 **FINAL MESSAGE**

* You don't need to be polite when someone crosses a line.

* You don't have to explain yourself.

* You don't owe anyone a photo, a hug, your attention, or your time.

* You are worthy of safety, respect, and care.

Always.

Chapter 16
You Don't Have to Earn It

You've unlearned some big things.

You've named the voices in your head.

You've said no when it felt scary.

You've started choosing you.

That is powerful work.

And it's only the beginning.

You don't have to perform to be worthy.

You don't have to chase approval to matter.

You don't have to earn rest, joy, love, or freedom.

You already deserve those things.

Just by being here.

JUST BY BEING YOU.

Celebrate this. Take a moment.

Look back at where you started - maybe confused, curious, unsure, or even nervous.

And now look at you.

You've done something not everyone dares to do:

- ✧ YOU'VE QUESTIONED THE RULES.
- ✧ YOU'VE SPOKEN UP.
- ✧ YOU'VE LET YOURSELF BE REAL.

That deserves celebration.

You've done amazing work - and you're just getting started.

KEEP GOING

You don't have to do this alone.

There are other girls doing this work too - some you know, some you don't (yet).

Talk to them. Share what you've learned. Start conversations that matter.

When it gets hard - and sometimes it will - you can take a break, ask for help, or return to the pages that reminded you who you are.

Being real is not something you have to figure out all by yourself.

Being real is something we do together.

⭐ FINAL REFLECTION

What is one thing you'll do differently now that you've done this work?

It could be something big, like speaking up more.

Or something small but powerful, like resting without feeling guilty.

Write it down. Whisper it to yourself. Share it with someone who sees the real you.

Let it be a little promise to yourself.

 WHAT'S NEXT?

This book doesn't really have a last page.

You can come back to it anytime, whenever something feels confusing, or when you just need a reminder of what's true.

Re-read the parts that spoke to you.

Redo the activities that helped.

Notice how you've changed.

And if something feels hard or heavy, you don't have to figure it out alone.

You can always talk to a trusted adult, teacher, or someone who makes you feel safe.

 THE FINAL WORD

- ✧ KEEP ASKING QUESTIONS.
- ✧ KEEP LISTENING IN.
- ✧ KEEP CHOOSING YOURSELF WITH KINDNESS.
- ✧ THE GOAL ISN'T TO BE PERFECT.
- ✧ THE GOAL IS TO BE FREE.

A Note From Us

Hey you,

Thank you for being here and for being curious, open, and brave enough to take this journey.

We wrote this book because we know what it's like to try so hard to be "good" and to feel like you have to shrink yourself to fit in. We also know how powerful it is when you start choosing yourself - your voice, your truth, your joy.

This book is just the beginning. You are already enough, just as you are. And we are so proud of you.

Keep being real. Keep being kind to yourself. And keep going - your way.

With love,

Caroline & Michelle

Acknowledgements

To **Lizzie** - thank you for your amazing drawings, your thoughtful sense-checking, and for helping us shape this book with care and creativity.

To **Carl** - thank you for all your encouragement and belief – so appreciated!

To **Oliver** - our very first beta reader (during your work experience!). Thank you for your honest, helpful feedback, especially in making sure it wasn't too *cringe*.

To **Tia** - thank you for your guidance on the book cover and helping us bring the visual identity to life.

To **James** - thank you for all your organising and encouragement - and your amazing editing abilities.

To all our brilliant beta readers -

Jessica, Sophia, Zara, Saar, Tilly, Caroline, Edith, Iris, Ida, and **Jessica** - thank you for reading early drafts, sharing your thoughts, and helping us shape something that feels real and relatable.

To the amazing grown-ups who supported them -

Sophie, Jen, Sanne, Laura, Alisa, Rachel, Rebecca, Becky and **Caroline** - we're so grateful for your time, trust, and encouragement.

To **Dee-Anne Tennent** – thank you for letting Caroline pick your teacher-brain and for your insights into what really lands in the classroom.

And finally, to every girl who picks up this book -

Thank you for your curiosity, your courage, and your questions.

We made this for you.

www.ingramcontent.com/pod-product-compliance
Lightning Source LLC
Chambersburg PA
CBHW041227070526
44584CB00006B/324